WHY DO RUDE PEOPLE PISS ME OFF!

HOW TO DEAL WITH DIFFICULT PEOPLE

MICHAEL T. BENNETT

"Luck is what happens when preparation meets opportunity"
— ATTRIBUTED TO ANCIENT ROMAN
PHILOSOPHER SENECA

TABLE OF CONTENTS

Keep the Momentum Going   ix

1. Introduction   1
2. What Really Gets Under Our Skin   6
3. Recognizing the Signs   13
4. Pause, Breathe, and then Respond   25
5. Using Humor as a Shield   35
6. Walking in Their Shoes   43
7. Building Emotional Resilience   50
8. Communication Skills   62
9. Mastering the Art of Letting Go   72
10. The Power of Positive Thinking   80
11. Setting Healthy Boundaries   90
12. Transformative Self-Reflection   98
13. Handling Rude Behavior Across Different Contexts   108
14. Helping Others Manage Rudeness   122
15. Finding Grace in Everyday Frustrations   135
16. Living a Life Free from the Annoyance of Rudeness   149
17. Conclusion   160

Thanks for Reading!   163
References   167

© Copyright 2024 - All rights reserved.

The content contained within this book may not be reproduced, duplicated or transmitted without direct written permission from the author or the publisher.

Under no circumstances will any blame or legal responsibility be held against the publisher, or author, for any damages, reparation, or monetary loss due to the information contained within this book, either directly or indirectly.

Legal Notice:

This book is copyright protected. It is only for personal use. You cannot amend, distribute, sell, use, quote or paraphrase any part, or the content within this book, without the consent of the author or publisher.

Disclaimer Notice:

Please note the information contained within this document is for educational and entertainment purposes only. All effort has been executed to present accurate, up to date, reliable, complete information. No warranties of any kind are declared or implied. Readers acknowledge that the author is not engaged in the rendering of legal, financial, medical or professional advice. The content within this book has been derived from various sources. Please consult a licensed professional before attempting any techniques outlined in this book.

By reading this document, the reader agrees that under no circumstances is the author responsible for any losses, direct or indirect, that are incurred as a result of the use of the information contained within this document, including, but not limited to, errors, omissions, or inaccuracies.

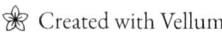 Created with Vellum

BONUS SECTION: READY TO TAKE THE NEXT STEP?

If you've made it this far, give yourself some credit, you're not just curious about why rude people get under your skin. You're ready to do something about it. And that's a big deal.

🎁 Claim a Free Mental Toughness Training Workbook

Need a space to work through your thoughts, triggers, and action steps? This workbook is packed with guided exercises and prompts to help you go deeper and get results that stick.

👉 **CLICK HERE**

Use it as your personal blueprint for staying calm, clear, and focused, no matter who or what tries to rattle you.

Keep the Momentum Going

If you want to support what we're doing here and take your journey even further:

☞ **Check out my second book,** to purchase my second book *Mental Toughness Training Made Simple*

My Second Book

☞ **To buy the Mental Toughness Training Companion Workbook** for Mental Toughness Training Made Simple:

The Companion Work Book

Keep the Momentum Going

Follow me on X @authormichaelt1

1

INTRODUCTION

"When dealing with people, remember you are not dealing with creatures of logic, but creatures of emotion." — Dale Carnegie

Why Do Rude People Piss Me Off! Hi, I'm Michael, and let me tell you, I know what it's like to struggle with dealing with difficult, rude people. I've been there more times than I can count. With a bachelor's degree from Towson University in Maryland and over 12 years as a retail manager for a multibillion-dollar company, I've seen it all. Teaching customer service standards is part of my life, so it drives me absolutely crazy when employees get paid to deliver crap service. Am I right?

Writing this book made me reflect deeply, and I realized something had to change, not just how I handle rude people but how I let them affect me. I know it sounds a bit wild, but I knew I needed to take control of how I react to other people's actions. It's not about changing them; it's about changing *me*.

Imagine this: You're in a bookstore, minding your own business, when you accidentally knock over a stack of books. A stranger nearby gives you a smug look and says, "Guess they don't teach spatial awareness in clumsiness school." Ouch, right? It feels like an invisible dart strikes you, causing a brief but sharp sting.

But here's the thing: Instead of letting it ruin your day, you smile and think, *"Well, if sarcasm burns calories, you're practically a fitness coach!"* With that witty comeback in mind, the sting fades, replaced by a sense of triumph. You didn't let the stranger's rude comment get under your skin. Instead, you turned it into a moment of lightness.

If you've ever let someone's snarky remark ruin your day, you're not alone. We've all faced rude comments from strangers, co-workers, or even friends. These interactions can be emotionally draining, leaving you wondering *why rude people piss you off* so much. But here's the truth: You can't control what others do, but you *can* control how you respond, and that's where this book comes in.

You might be thinking, "How can I handle rude people without losing my temper?" The answer lies in humor, empathy, and resilience. Imagine someone cutting in front of you while you're waiting in line. Instead of fuming, you picture them frantically searching for the last doughnut, and suddenly, it's hard to take them seriously. Humor, though it might seem unconventional, is a powerful tool when dealing with rudeness. It diffuses tension and helps you maintain emotional balance. Instead of letting a rude comment derail your day, you can turn it into something to laugh about, keeping your outlook positive and your peace intact.

This book is about taking control of your reactions, finding calm amid the chaos, and yes, maybe even having a good laugh along the way. You'll learn how to use humor to deflect tension, build empathy to understand where rudeness comes from, and develop resilience to bounce back stronger from difficult interactions. Along the way, we'll dive into practical strategies like assertive communication, setting boundaries, and prioritizing self-care.

By the end, you'll be equipped to handle life's annoyances with grace and confidence. So, whether you're dealing with a problematic co-worker, a rude customer, or just the everyday frustrations of life, this book will give you the tools to stay calm, respond thoughtfully, and turn those rude moments into opportunities for growth.

Let's get started on transforming how you handle rudeness, one smile at a time!

Why Humor, Empathy, and Resilience Matter

This book isn't just about controlling your reactions—it's about thriving in the face of rudeness with humor, compassion, and strength. You'll learn to see the absurdity in others' behavior and use that perspective to reduce your stress. Laughter not only helps you cope, but it also strengthens your emotional stability. By the end of this journey, you'll be able to handle life's annoyances with a smile—or maybe even a good chuckle.

But humor is just one tool in your toolkit. Imagine being able to transform your initial anger into calmness. Throughout these chapters, you'll learn practical strategies for effectively managing rudeness. Whether it's taking a deep breath before responding or using assertive communication to set boundaries, these techniques will empower you to handle difficult interactions with confidence and grace.

Building Empathy: Understanding That Rudeness Isn't About You

One of the pivotal approaches we'll explore is empathy. Recognizing that everyone has tough days can help you avoid taking their rudeness personally. Often, rudeness stems from a person's internal struggles rather than anything related to you. Imagine being able to recognize this in the heat of the moment—it can completely change how you react. By considering the other person's perspective, you'll respond with more calmness and compassion, defusing the situation before it escalates.

Prioritizing Self-Care: Your Secret Weapon

In addition to humor and empathy, this book will dive into the importance of self-care. When you focus on your own mental and emotional well-being, you're better equipped to handle life's challenges without feeling overwhelmed. We'll explore mindfulness techniques, the importance of sleep, and how engaging in activities you love can bolster your resilience. Self-care isn't just a luxury—it's essential for managing stress and staying emotionally strong in the face of rudeness.

Assertive Communication: Setting Boundaries with Confidence

We'll also discuss the art of assertive communication. Expressing your thoughts and needs clearly and respectfully can significantly enhance your ability to handle rude encounters. By setting firm boundaries and standing up for yourself in a calm, controlled manner, you can prevent situations from escalating and protect your emotional well-being. Assertiveness doesn't mean being confrontational; it means respecting yourself enough to communicate your needs with clarity.

Building Emotional Resilience: Bouncing Back Stronger

Lastly, we'll explore the power of building emotional resilience. Resilience is the ability to stay strong during challenges and quickly bounce back from adversity. Developing resilience will help you manage rudeness more effectively and become more adaptable in navigating life's ups and downs. But this journey isn't just about surviving rude encounters—it's about thriving and becoming stronger with every challenge you face, especially when dealing with difficult people.

The Payoff: A More Peaceful, Happier You

Picture this: By learning how to manage rudeness, you're not just getting through the day—you're becoming a stronger, more graceful person. Imagine how every part of your life could improve! Your relationships grow because you're better at handling conflict. Your stress levels decrease because you're not letting every rude comment get under your skin. Most importantly, you feel happier and healthier because you're spending more time enjoying life and less time feeling frustrated.

This book will guide you through that transformation. We'll share real-life examples, practical advice, and plenty of humor to help you shift how you respond to rudeness. You'll discover new ways to cope with difficult situations and build the emotional resilience needed to thrive.

Whether you're dealing with a problematic co-worker, a rude customer, or life's everyday challenges, this book has something for you. It's time to take control of how you react to rudeness and turn those frustrating moments into opportunities for growth—and even a good laugh. Ready to start this journey? Let's jump in and transform how you handle rudeness, one smile at a time.

2

WHAT REALLY GETS UNDER OUR SKIN

"How people treat you is their karma; how you react is yours." — Wayne Dyer

When someone like my employee John snaps at me for no reason, it feels like a punch to the gut. Dealing with difficult people always catches me off guard, like a sudden downpour on a sunny day. One minute I'm fine, and the next, I'm left wondering, "Wait... what just happened? Did I do something wrong?" I try to keep things easygoing, so when someone's rude out of nowhere, it feels personal, like they've gone out of their way to mess up my day.

Let's be honest: it's hard to just shake it off. That moment sticks with me, replaying in my mind as I try to figure out what I did to deserve it. Whether it's a stranger's cutting remark or a co-worker's sharp tone, these encounters can leave us feeling frustrated and drained. But why does it hit so hard?

Here's the thing: it's not just about what was said, it's about how it makes me feel, like I've been disrespected for no reason. And you probably feel the same way. Rudeness throws us off balance, makes us second-guess ourselves, and leaves a lingering frustration.

This is where mindset becomes crucial. Wayne Dyer's quote reminds me that while I can't control how others treat me, I *can* control how I react. That's easier said than done, right? But it's empowering once you get the hang of it. Every rude comment, every dismissive tone, presents a choice: I can either let it ruin my mood or decide that their behavior is about *them*, not me.

This chapter dives into the psychology behind why rudeness stings so much. Understanding what's going on in our minds when we face difficult people can give us the tools to handle it better. What if we could stop rudeness from getting under our skin in the first place? Imagine feeling more in control, less shaken, and more confident when these moments arise.

Let's explore why these encounters affect us so deeply and learn how to take charge of our reactions. By the end of this chapter, you'll feel more equipped to handle difficult people with grace and resilience.

Rude Behavior Unpacked: What's Going On?

Rude behavior hits us hard because it taps into several deep psychological and emotional triggers. Whether we realize it or not, much of our response stems from how we see ourselves and others.

One of the biggest reasons rudeness stings is *social comparison*. We naturally measure our worth by comparing ourselves to those around us. When someone is rude, it can feel like a direct threat to our self-esteem. Think about a time when a co-worker rudely dismissed your idea during a meeting. It's not just about the comment—it's about feeling like your abilities are being questioned, making you doubt yourself and your standing in the group.

Rudeness also triggers *cognitive dissonance*. We want to believe in mutual respect, but encountering rudeness forces us to confront the gap between what we expect and what we get. This clash can cause stress and frustration because it disrupts the way we believe people should behave. It's like a sour note in a song you thought would be perfect.

Then there's *emotional contagion*. When we encounter or witness rudeness, those negative emotions can spread like wildfire, dragging down our mood and making us react poorly in future interactions. It's a cycle: one person's rudeness can create tension that ripples through a workplace, a family, or even a group of friends. We often pass that negativity on without realizing it.

Lastly, *lack of empathy* plays a huge role. Rudeness often stems from someone not considering how their behavior affects others. When someone is rude, it sends the message that your feelings don't matter—and that can feel deeply hurtful. For example, a sarcastic response from a teacher or a friend can make you feel small and undervalued. This lack of empathy breaks down relationships and leaves us feeling disconnected.

The good news? Recognizing what's happening inside can help us take back control. With a little mindfulness and emotional resilience, we can stop these cycles of negativity before they take over.

Cultural and Societal Norms

Rudeness hits us hard because our reactions are shaped by cultural norms and societal expectations. Let's break down a few key factors.

First, *norms of politeness* vary between cultures. In some places, politeness is a must, like bowing in Japan to show respect. In other cultures, like the U.S., directness can be valued over formalities. So, what feels rude to one person might just be straightforward to another. Your background heavily influences how you interpret these interactions.

Then there's *collective identity*. Rudeness isn't just about you; it can reflect on your whole group. If someone from your community behaves rudely in public, it can feel like an embarrassment to everyone. This shared sense of responsibility makes the sting of rudeness feel even sharper.

Media also plays a role. Rudeness is often normalized in TV, movies, and online content. Seeing rude behavior treated as funny or acceptable can dull our shock but build long-term frustration. It's easy to get used to it, but the constant exposure doesn't make it any easier to deal with.

Generational differences add another layer. Older generations, raised with strict social etiquette, might see today's relaxed norms as rude. Younger people, used to casual online interactions, might see the same behavior as normal or assertive. These generational gaps create tension when people's expectations around politeness don't match up.

Ultimately, *societal expectations* shape what we see as respectful or rude. From a young age, we're taught how to behave through cultural cues and lessons from family and teachers. When someone acts rudely, it clashes with the norms we've internalized, making it feel like a personal attack.

Personal Triggers and Insecurities

Rudeness can hit us where we're most vulnerable, triggering deep emotional reactions. Let's break down why that happens and how we can manage it.

First, *self-esteem* plays a huge role. When someone's rude, it can fuel our own doubts about ourselves. If we already feel insecure about something—like our work—a rude comment can feel like confirmation of those fears. That's why it hurts so much. To handle this, we need to build our self-worth so it doesn't depend on what others think. Reminding ourselves of our strengths can help create a buffer against rude behavior.

Next, there's the *fear of rejection*. Rudeness often feels like someone is pushing us away, triggering that primal need for acceptance. We all want to feel like we belong, so when someone is rude, it feels like a personal rejection. To cope, try asking yourself, "Am I taking this too personally?" Remember, rudeness says more about them than it does about you.

Another big factor is *past trauma*. If you've been through experiences like bullying or rejection, even small slights can bring up those old wounds. It's important to work through these past hurts—whether through therapy, mindfulness, or just talking it out with someone you trust. Separating past pain from the present helps keep things in perspective.

Unmet expectations also trigger us. We all have standards for how we expect others to behave. When someone acts rudely, it breaks those unwritten rules, which can feel like a personal attack. The key is understanding that not everyone shares your expectations. Communicating calmly and clearly can help avoid misunderstandings and set better boundaries.

At the end of the day, these emotional triggers remind us of our need for respect and acceptance. By recognizing and managing these triggers, we can build emotional resilience—not by ignoring rude behavior, but by responding in ways that protect our mental health. And it helps to remember that rudeness often comes from the other person's struggles, not a reflection of our worth.

For those who deal with rudeness frequently—like customer service reps or teachers—having ways to stay positive is crucial. Stress relief, peer support, and even humor can be powerful tools. Finding humor in these moments creates distance from the negativity, letting you laugh instead of letting it get under your skin.

The Influence of Early Experiences

Our early life experiences play a huge role in how we perceive and respond to rudeness. Childhood environments, modeled behaviors, and social conditioning all shape our emotional reactions.

If we grew up in a household where respect was shown, we likely carry those values into adulthood. On the flip side, if rudeness or disrespect was common, we might be more desensitized to it or even mimic those behaviors ourselves. A child who sees their parents handle conflicts calmly is more likely to adopt that same approach, while a child who witnesses constant yelling may believe that's how disagreements should be handled.

Modeling behavior teaches us a lot about how to respond to rudeness. If the adults around us manage rude behavior assertively and calmly, we learn to do the same. But if we see aggressive or passive responses, those habits can stick with us into adulthood.

Social conditioning also plays a big part. Schools, for example, can either enforce respectful behavior or, if they ignore bullying, teach kids that rudeness is acceptable. The media adds to this, sometimes glorifying rude behavior, which can blur the lines between what's acceptable and what's not.

Finally, our *coping mechanisms* for handling rudeness often come from what we saw growing up. Those taught to be assertive can navigate rude encounters without escalating tensions. Others might struggle with finding a balanced approach.

To better cope, empathy and emotional regulation are key. Try to understand why someone might be rude—maybe they're having a bad day. Practicing empathy helps diffuse situations. Also, learning to regulate your emotions can keep you calm in the face of rudeness, making it easier to respond with grace.

Insights and Implications

Understanding why rudeness affects us so deeply can help us manage our reactions better. We've looked at how things like social comparison, cognitive dissonance, emotional contagion, and empathy play a big role in how we respond when someone is rude. Recognizing these factors can help us realize that our discomfort often comes from deeper psychological and cultural influences. Once we become aware of these triggers, we can start building strategies to handle rude encounters with more strength and calm. Practicing self-affirmation, developing empathy, and working through past experiences can make a real difference.

Knowing that societal expectations and our personal insecurities also shape how we react gives us a clearer sense of why rudeness can feel so jarring. Our early experiences and the environments we grew up in set the foundation for how we perceive and deal with disrespect. With this understanding, we can focus on healthier ways to cope, whether it's through mindfulness, open communication, or simply taking a breath before responding. By reinforcing our self-worth and learning not to take others' negativity personally, we can create a more balanced emotional response to rudeness—and feel better overall.

Reflections

When someone's rudeness shakes your confidence, what does it reveal about your own triggers, and how can understanding those triggers empower you to respond with strength and grace?

I've realized that dealing with difficult people, especially when they're rude, can affect me on a much deeper level than I usually acknowledge. When someone is rude, it feels like a personal attack, shaking my self-worth and causing emotional discomfort. I've noticed how negative emotions from these encounters can spread quickly, impacting my mood and interactions with others throughout the day. Personal triggers, like past experiences or low self-esteem, make it even harder to brush off rude behavior.

Understanding this has shown me the importance of building emotional resilience and empathy—not just to protect myself, but to rise above the negative effects of dealing with difficult people and their disrespectful behavior.

Now that we've explored why rudeness hits so hard, it's time to dive deeper into the specific triggers behind it. Recognizing what sparks rude behavior in both yourself and others can help you handle these situations with more calm and control. Let's dig into the common triggers of dealing with difficult people and explore ways to manage them effectively.

3
RECOGNIZING THE SIGNS

"Between stimulus and response, there is a space. In that space is our power to choose our response. In our response lies our growth and our freedom."
— Viktor Frankl

If you haven't read *Man's Search for Meaning* by Viktor Frankl, I can't recommend it enough. It's a short but profound read that has shaped the way I see life. Frankl's insights on finding meaning, even in the most challenging situations, taught me a crucial lesson: while we can't control what happens to us, we can always control how we respond.

I remember a couple of years ago, sitting in a meeting, trying to contribute to the discussion. But every time I opened my mouth, my colleague, interrupted me. At first, I shrugged it off, telling myself it wasn't a big deal. But by the fifth interruption, frustration was bubbling up, and staying calm felt like an uphill battle. That's when it hit me. The real issue wasn't just that he was cutting me off. It was the deeper feeling of being dismissed. It felt like an unspoken message: *What you're saying doesn't matter.*

Recognizing that trigger changed everything. Instead of snapping back or stewing in silence, I paused, took a breath, and calmly redirected the conversation. It wasn't easy, but that small shift turned what could've been a heated argument into a productive discussion.

Moments like this have taught me an essential truth: frustration often stems from emotional triggers, not just rude behavior itself. When we can identify those triggers, whether it's feeling ignored, disrespected, or undervalued, we can start to take back control. And trust me, once you start noticing them, your reactions will begin to transform.

We've all had those everyday moments when frustration creeps in. A car cuts you off, a snarky email lands in your inbox, or someone drops a passive-aggressive comment at the dinner table. The key is learning to spot these triggers before they hijack your emotions. By pinpointing what sets you off, you can respond more thoughtfully and keep your cool, even when dealing with difficult people.

Let's face it, life is full of assholes. But with a little self-awareness and the right tools, you'll be ready to handle them with grace, confidence, and maybe even a little humor.

Common Scenarios That Evoke Frustration

Recognizing what sets off your emotions when you're faced with rude behavior is key to understanding why you react the way you do. By spotting those triggers, you can start to see patterns in how you respond, which gives you the chance to manage your reactions better and protect your emotional well-being.

Office Interactions

The workplace is a common source of frustration, especially when dealing with dismissive colleagues or rude clients. Imagine spending hours perfecting a presentation, only to have a colleague brush it off without even looking, or a client interrupting you mid-meeting. It's not just your work being challenged—it's your sense of worth and competence.

What makes these situations even more aggravating is the underlying message of disrespect. When a colleague cuts you off, it feels like they're saying your voice doesn't matter. Recognizing this emotional trigger helps you step back, understand why it bothers you, and decide how to respond thoughtfully. Maybe you'll address it calmly or choose to manage your emotions internally instead.

Dealing with rude behavior at work often means setting clear boundaries. By recognizing patterns and developing strategies, you can protect your emotional well-being without letting the situation escalate.

Public Spaces

Rude behavior in public places like grocery stores or public transport can really get under your skin. Picture waiting patiently in line at the store, only to have someone cut right in front of you without even acknowledging your presence. It's frustrating because, in public spaces, people often feel no accountability and act rudely, knowing they likely won't face any consequences.

Recognizing that this behavior often comes from the impersonal nature of these environments can help you emotionally detach. Public spaces tend to be chaotic, with people rushing and dealing with their own frustrations. By mentally preparing for these encounters, you can handle them more easily. For example, when you're in a busy grocery line, expect that someone might be inconsiderate, but commit to staying calm and not letting it ruin your day.

Online Interactions

With its anonymity and lack of face-to-face accountability, the digital world can easily become a breeding ground for rudeness. Social media, comment sections, and even emails can quickly turn hostile. One simple post might attract negative comments, or a short email could come across as unnecessarily harsh.

Recognizing that the anonymity of the internet makes it easier for people to be rude can help you detach from the negativity. Remember, online rudeness usually says more about the person behind the comment than about you. By setting boundaries for your online interactions—whether that means limiting screen time or blocking negative individuals—you can protect your mental health. Don't hesitate to step away from the screen when needed and remind yourself that not every comment deserves your attention.

Family Dynamics

Rudeness within families can sting more than in any other setting. A dismissive remark from a sibling or parent hurts deeply because we expect our family to be our main source of love and support. When they act rudely, it feels more like a personal betrayal.

Families often have complex dynamics, and changing long-established patterns can be tough. Recognizing these patterns is key to understanding why certain family members behave this way. For example, a sibling who constantly belittles you might be reacting to unresolved childhood issues, or a parent's dismissive attitude could stem from their own insecurities.

Dealing with rudeness in the family usually means setting clear boundaries, even though it can feel uncomfortable. If a family member's behavior consistently hurts you, it's important to let them know how their actions affect you and create boundaries that protect your emotional well-being.

Recognizing Triggers

Whether it happens at work, in public, online, or even with family, rude behavior can spark strong emotional reactions. These responses often come from feeling disrespected, inadequate, or even betrayed. But once you recognize what's triggering these emotions, you can manage them more effectively and keep rude behavior from taking a toll on your well-being.

Building emotional resilience means spotting patterns in how you react. It doesn't mean rude behavior won't affect you anymore—it's bound to—but you'll be more prepared to handle it in a way that protects your mental health. Instead of acting on impulse, you can pause, take a moment to reflect, and choose how you want to respond.

We all deal with rude behavior from time to time, but knowing your triggers gives you the confidence to manage those moments with more control. Now that you've identified your emotional triggers, it's time to focus on one of the most important tools for managing rude behavior: setting personal boundaries. Understanding how to set and communicate boundaries can shield you from emotional harm and help ensure more respectful interactions. Let's dive into how to define and communicate your boundaries effectively.

Understanding Personal Boundaries

Personal boundaries are essential for protecting your emotional, physical, and mental well-being. They act as invisible lines that define what's okay and what's not, ensuring you feel safe and respected in your interactions. When your boundaries are clear, they create healthy spaces and reduce frustration, especially when dealing with rude or disrespectful behavior.

Defining Your Boundaries

Your boundaries are unique to you, shaped by your experiences, values, and comfort levels. The first step in defining them is self-awareness. Think about times when you've felt uncomfortable, disrespected, or upset, those are likely moments when someone crossed a boundary. Maybe you feel uneasy when someone invades your personal space or makes comments about your appearance.

Here are a few key types of boundaries:

- **Emotional boundaries**: These protect you from being overwhelmed by others' emotions or negativity. For example, if someone constantly dumps their problems on you, it might be a sign to set an emotional boundary.
- **Physical boundaries**: These involve personal space and touch, like preferring to keep a certain distance during conversations or feeling uncomfortable with casual hugs from acquaintances.
- **Verbal boundaries**: These are about how people speak to or about you. If someone frequently uses harsh language or

makes inappropriate jokes, it may be time to set clearer verbal boundaries.
- **Time boundaries**: These manage how much time you give to others. If you're overcommitted, setting time boundaries can help you preserve your energy and personal space.

Everyone's boundaries are different, and what feels right for one person might not for another. Recognizing this helps foster empathy and respect in your relationships.

Recognizing When Someone Crosses Your Boundaries

It can be tough to spot when someone has crossed your boundary, but it's important for protecting your emotional well-being. Some common signs include:

- Feeling uneasy or stressed after an interaction.
- Sensing that you've been taken advantage of or disrespected.
- Noticing a consistent pattern of discomfort with specific behaviors.

When these feelings arise, take a moment to reflect on *why* the behavior bothers you. Does it clash with your values, or is it triggering a past negative experience? Understanding the root cause will help you express your boundaries more clearly.

For example, if a colleague frequently interrupts you in meetings, leaving you feeling ignored, this may signal that your need for respectful communication isn't being met. Once you understand why it affects you, you'll be in a better position to address it.

Communicating Your Boundaries

Expressing your boundaries can feel intimidating, but it's crucial to ensure they're respected. Clear, assertive communication is key. Here are a few strategies to help

Be direct: Clearly explain the behavior that's bothering you. For example, "I feel disrespected when you interrupt me during meetings. Please let me finish before responding."

- **Use "I" statements:** Talk about how *you* feel without blaming the other person. Instead of pointing fingers, say, "I feel uncomfortable when people make personal comments about my appearance."
- **Set consequences:** If someone continues to cross your boundaries, let them know what will happen next. For instance, "If the interruptions continue, I'll need to bring this up with our supervisor."

Communicating your boundaries doesn't always bring instant change, but standing firm sends a clear message that your limits matter. Some people might resist, but consistency helps reinforce the importance of respecting your boundaries.

Challenges in Setting Boundaries

Setting boundaries can be tough, especially with people you're close to or when it feels confrontational. Some common challenges include:

- **Guilt or fear:** Many people hesitate to set boundaries because they're afraid of offending others. It's important to remember that prioritizing your well-being isn't selfish—it's necessary.
- **Cultural norms:** In some cultures, assertiveness is discouraged, making it harder to express your needs clearly. This can add another layer of difficulty when setting boundaries.
- **Manipulation:** Some people might try to guilt-trip you into relaxing your boundaries by saying things like, "I was only joking," or "You're too sensitive." Recognizing these tactics can help you stay firm.

In tough situations, it's important to practice self-compassion and be patient with yourself. Don't hesitate to reach out to trusted friends, mentors, or therapists for support as you work on setting and maintaining boundaries.

Maintaining Boundaries in Difficult Situations

Enforcing boundaries can be tricky, especially in confrontational situations or with people you're close to. If someone tries to guilt-trip you, calmly restate your boundary by saying something like, "I understand how you feel, but I'm uncomfortable with that behavior, and I need you to respect that."

Practicing boundary-setting with a trusted friend can also help you feel more confident when it's time for those honest conversations. And remember, setting boundaries isn't about being harsh, it's about protecting your well-being and building healthier relationships.

Moving Forward With Confidence

Setting boundaries not only improves your emotional well-being but also strengthens your relationships. When your boundaries are respected, you'll find yourself feeling less frustrated and more at peace. Over time, it gets easier to reinforce your boundaries, and others will come to understand that they're non-negotiable.

Now that you see how setting boundaries protects you from rudeness, let's shift gears and talk about stress and fatigue. These external pressures can heavily influence how you respond to rudeness and emotional triggers. Up next, we'll explore how managing stress can help you build emotional resilience and stay balanced in tough situations.

The Role of Stress and Fatigue

We all have moments when stress or fatigue makes dealing with rude behavior feel impossible. It's so important to understand how stress and tiredness affect your emotional resilience because when you're feeling drained, even small annoyances can feel like personal attacks. But don't worry—you can regain control and protect your well-being with a few mindful steps.

Why Do Rude People Piss Me Off!

The first step is recognizing what triggers your stress. Maybe it's the pressure of tight deadlines, a long commute, or a series of back-to-back meetings. Keeping a journal for a week can help you spot patterns. You might realize it's your workload or a lack of clear communication from your boss that pushes you to the edge. Or maybe those afternoon meetings leave you so drained that you become more sensitive to rudeness later in the day. These little insights are so valuable because they help you understand where your stress is coming from, so you can start managing it better.

Fatigue plays a big role too. When you're sleep-deprived, your ability to handle emotions weakens, and even minor annoyances can feel overwhelming. We've all been there—on days when you're well-rested, it's easy to brush off rude comments, but when you're running on empty, small slights can feel like much bigger issues. By prioritizing sleep—creating a regular routine, cutting back on caffeine, and stepping away from screens before bed—you'll notice a huge improvement in your emotional resilience.

Managing stress and fatigue isn't about perfection, but it's about small, steady changes that make a big difference. Try adding some deep breathing or a few minutes of meditation into your routine when you're feeling overwhelmed. Even a short walk or a little stretching can boost your mood and help release the tension that builds up during the day.

Setting boundaries, both at work and at home, is also crucial. If you're someone who says "yes" to everything, learning to say "no" can be a game-changer for protecting your time and energy. By clearly communicating your limits, you'll prevent overwhelm before it starts. And don't forget the basics—stay hydrated and eat well. When you skip meals or forget to drink water, your irritability can increase, making it even harder to stay calm when facing rude behavior.

Don't underestimate the power of social support, either. Talking to a friend, family member, or colleague who really understands can be incredibly comforting. Sometimes, just knowing you're not alone in facing stress can make it feel more manageable.

Self-reflection is a powerful tool here too. Take note of the times when you feel most stressed or tired. Is it late afternoon meetings that drain your energy? Is it a specific person whose behavior spikes your stress? Keeping a journal or using an app to track these moments can help you build a plan that works for *you*.

For example, I used to feel completely wiped out after late meetings, and I would snap at people without even realizing it. Over time, I realized it wasn't just the meetings—it was my energy levels at that time of day. So, I made a small change: I started scheduling important meetings earlier in the day when I felt more energized. And when a colleague constantly stressed me out, I had a tough but honest conversation to set some boundaries. It wasn't easy, but it helped, and little by little, I started feeling more in control. It's still a work in progress, but these small changes really do add up.

Now that we've looked at how stress and fatigue play a role in how we handle rudeness, it's also important to recognize how past experiences shape our reactions. Unresolved issues from previous encounters can heighten our sensitivity to rude behavior, but by understanding these patterns, we can start building emotional resilience and respond to rude behavior with more ease.

Let's explore how your past influences your present reactions and work on turning those experiences into tools for growth.

The Impact of Previous Negative Experiences

Past experiences heavily influence how we respond to rudeness today. If you've been belittled or dismissed before, it's natural to carry those feelings with you. It's like lugging around emotional baggage—unresolved hurts that spill out when a similar situation arises. This can lead to overreacting to minor slights, as you're not just responding to the present but to past wounds as well.

Your brain creates associations between past and present experiences, so if you've been interrupted in the past, a similar situation might trigger a stronger emotional response. Recognizing these connections is key to managing them. Processing past hurts can reduce their grip on you, and journaling can be a helpful way to reflect and untangle your emotions.

Cognitive behavioral therapy (CBT) can also help reframe negative thoughts and manage your emotional reactions. Meditation, on the other hand, keeps you focused on the present, helping you avoid dwelling on past pain. Even taking a deep breath before responding to rudeness can make a big difference.

Reframing past rude encounters as opportunities for growth is powerful. Each experience teaches resilience, patience, and understanding. Positive self-talk, like reminding yourself "I've handled this before," can boost your confidence in difficult moments.

Sharing your experiences with friends or support groups can provide comfort and new perspectives. Building a strong support network helps lighten the emotional load of dealing with rudeness.

It's also important to remember that rude behavior often stems from the other person's stress or insecurity. Understanding this allows you to detach emotionally and not take their behavior personally. While you don't have to tolerate rudeness, this realization helps protect your self-esteem.

Finally, having a range of coping strategies—whether journaling, physical activity, or using humor—can help you manage stress and frustration. Handling rudeness with grace comes from understanding the emotional triggers beneath the surface, and with self-reflection, therapy, or support, you can build resilience and protect your well-being.

Reflections

What emotional triggers affect you the most when faced with rudeness, and how can recognizing them help you respond with greater calm and control?

As I reflected on my emotional triggers, I realized how recognizing them can help me stay calm in the face of rude behavior. I've noticed that rudeness at work often leaves me feeling undervalued, while in public spaces, it's easier to brush things off because it feels more impersonal. Online interactions, with their anonymity, tend to bring out harshness, but setting boundaries has helped me protect my well-being. Family is where emotions run deepest, and I've learned that clear communication and setting limits are essential for avoiding frustration.

I've also recognized that I'm more sensitive to rudeness when I'm stressed or tired, making it harder to manage my emotions in those moments. Knowing this has been a game-changer in understanding how to handle these situations better.

Now that you've recognized your own triggers, it's time to shift the focus to how you respond in the moment. While your initial reaction may come quickly, taking a pause before you react can make all the difference. Next, let's explore how something as simple as taking a deep breath can help you regain control and handle rudeness with grace.

4

PAUSE, BREATHE, AND THEN RESPOND

"Feelings are much like waves, we can't stop them from coming, but we can choose which one to surf." — Jonatan Mårtensson

Emotions have a way of sneaking up on us, like waves crashing on the shore. One moment, you're enjoying the view; the next, you're bracing yourself against a surge of frustration. I'm sitting at my friends sons baseball game, trying to savor the moment, when the parent next to me starts loudly criticizing the teams pitcher, my friends son. My frustration starts to bubble, each word feeling like a jab. But instead of letting it overwhelm me, I pause.

I take a deep breath, count to five, and let their words fade into the background. In that brief moment of stillness, I realize something important: I don't have to ride this wave of frustration. Their negativity doesn't need to become my problem. I smile to myself, proud that I've stayed calm. When the game ends, I walk away with my head held high, knowing I didn't let their rudeness ruin my day.

Sometimes, something as simple as taking a breath is enough to regain control and choose a better wave to surf. But what if we could take this a step further? Let's explore how visualizing calm can make this practice even more powerful, helping you navigate life's choppy waters with confidence and grace.

Visualization Techniques for Mental Reframing

Visualization is a powerful tool for handling stress, especially when dealing with difficult people—like a rude colleague. Instead of reacting on impulse, you can use mental imagery to shift how you see the situation and respond more thoughtfully. Picture it: rather than snapping back, you take a deep breath and imagine handling the conversation calmly and constructively.

Research shows that visualizing positive outcomes helps you stay in control of your emotions and handle conflicts more effectively (Davis, 2023). For example, if you mentally rehearse a calm, respectful conversation with someone who upset you, it prepares your brain to approach the real situation with more grace, helping you avoid those knee-jerk reactions.

Visualizing Positive Outcomes

One helpful way to manage rude behavior is to imagine a more optimistic outcome where both parties stay calm. For example, let's say your colleague, Mark, rudely dismisses your input during a meeting. Instead of letting frustration get the best of you, picture a conversation where you both calmly discuss the issue and find common ground. This shift from expecting conflict to focusing on resolution helps calm your emotions and gives you more clarity.

Research backs this up: studies show that visualizing positive outcomes reduces stress and increases empathy, making it easier to manage conflicts (Smith, 2018). When you mentally prepare for things to go well, you set yourself up to handle real-life situations with more confidence and success.

Creating Mental Distance

Another helpful visualization technique is creating emotional distance from the situation. Often, our gut reaction to rudeness comes from feeling personally attacked. But by imagining the problem as if you're watching it unfold on a movie screen, you can detach from that emotional charge. For instance, if Sarah from accounting makes a snide comment, try visualizing the situation as if you're observing it from the outside, like a third person watching a scene play out.

This technique helps you see the situation without being pulled into the emotions of it, making it easier to stay composed. Research shows that mentally distancing yourself in stressful situations lowers emotional reactivity and helps you respond more calmly (Shpancer, 2020). It gives you that extra space to choose a thoughtful response instead of reacting on impulse.

Crafting Empowering Mental Imagery

Dealing with rude behavior can leave you feeling powerless or overwhelmed, but using empowering mental imagery helps you take back emotional control. Imagine yourself in a peaceful setting—like a serene beach or a quiet forest—whenever you're in a stressful situation. For example, when an unreasonable client is stressing you out, mentally shift to this calming place to keep yourself balanced.

Pairing this visualization with deep breathing makes it even more effective. Research shows that this kind of imagery can significantly lower stress and boost emotional resilience, helping you stay calm under pressure (NeuroLaunch Editorial Team, 2024).

Visualizing Compassion

Another powerful technique is visualizing compassion. Instead of getting defensive when someone is rude, try imagining that the person might be dealing with their own struggles. For example, if your team leader, Josh, snaps at you during a project review, picture him having a rough day—maybe he's dealing with personal stress. This shift in perspective helps you respond with patience instead of frustration.

By visualizing compassion, you help de-escalate tense situations and foster a more empathetic mindset. Research shows that empathy-driven visualization can lead to more positive outcomes, reducing emotional reactivity and promoting understanding (Baer, 2017).

Applying Visualization in Daily Routines

To make visualization a regular practice:

1. Start your day by mentally rehearsing positive interactions.
2. Visualize successful conversations and peaceful exchanges before any potentially stressful encounters arise.
3. When a difficult situation occurs, apply one of these visualization techniques—imagining a positive outcome, creating distance, or visualizing a peaceful setting.

These methods help break the cycle of stress, giving you the chance to engage thoughtfully rather than reacting on pure emotion. Now that you've learned how to use visualization to stay calm during stressful encounters, let's dive into another powerful strategy: breathing techniques. We'll explore how simple, mindful breathing can help you regain control and respond to rudeness with clarity and calm.

Breathing Strategies

Regulating your breath is a simple way to quickly regain calm during stressful situations. Different techniques can shift an emotional reaction into a thoughtful response, making it easier to manage stress.

- **Deep belly breathing**: This technique focuses on breathing deeply from the diaphragm. Place one hand on your chest and the other on your belly. Inhale deeply through your nose, letting your belly rise more than your chest, then slowly exhale through your mouth. This method triggers the body's relaxation response, lowering stress levels instantly—perfect for managing tough moments, like dealing with a challenging client.
- **Box breathing**: Also known as square breathing, this structured technique helps you regain control. Inhale for four seconds, hold for four, exhale for four, and hold again for four. Repeat the cycle. It's discreet and can calm your nerves quickly, whether you're at your desk or in a meeting.

- **Breath visualization**: Pair deep breathing with mental imagery. As you inhale, imagine calm waves washing over you; as you exhale, picture tension leaving your body. It engages both body and mind, making it great for those who enjoy using their imagination.
- **Counting breaths**: When you feel frustrated, count each inhale and exhale. For example, inhale on "one," exhale on "two," and continue until you reach ten. This keeps your focus on your breath and away from stress.

Practicing these techniques regularly makes them second nature, so you're ready to stay composed in stressful situations. Apps like Headspace can also help guide you through these exercises if you need extra support.

Counting to Ten

When you're confronted with rudeness, it's easy to react in the heat of the moment. Strong emotions can push us to say or do things we might regret later. That's where the simple act of counting to ten comes in. It gives you a moment to pause, gather your thoughts, and respond more thoughtfully. This technique helps you regain control, leading to more respectful and constructive interactions, even in tough situations.

Immediate Impulse Control

When someone is rude, it's natural to want to defend yourself or snap back. But counting to ten can be a simple way to create a pause and stop that automatic reaction. It gives you just enough time to step back, take a breath, and choose a more thoughtful response. This pause can help prevent conflicts from escalating and keeps your emotions in check.

Imagine working at a customer service desk when an angry customer starts yelling. It's easy to feel defensive, but by counting to ten, you can transition from reacting to responding calmly. In those moments, you remind yourself that their frustration is likely about the product, not you personally. Instead of lashing out, you handle their concerns with calm professionalism, which often defuses the tension.

Creating Emotional Space

Counting to ten also helps create emotional space between you and the rude behavior. Strong emotions can cloud your judgment, but giving yourself a moment to recover helps reduce the intensity of your reaction. It lets you stay composed and in control.

For example, in a recent meeting, a colleague brushed off my suggestion, and I immediately felt anger rising. My first instinct was to snap back, feeling frustrated and undervalued. But I paused and counted to ten. In that moment, I reminded myself that one dismissive comment doesn't define my worth. Taking that quick pause allowed me to respond calmly and keep the conversation productive, rather than letting it spiral out of control.

Adding Playful Variations

To make counting to ten more engaging, try adding playful variations. You could count in a different language, which distracts your mind from the frustration and shifts your focus. If you're learning a new language, this doubles as a chance to practice while giving you a mental break from the situation. By the time you reach ten, you'll likely feel less attached to the anger and more in control.

You can also count backward from ten or in increments (like 2, 4, 6...) to keep your brain active and focused. For example, if a friend's rude comment irritates you, counting backward might provide just enough of a distraction to help you avoid reacting impulsively. It gives you the space to respond thoughtfully and with a clearer mind.

Pairing With Self-Reflection

Counting to ten becomes even more powerful when you pair it with a moment of self-reflection. After counting, ask yourself: *Why did that comment bother me? How do I want to respond in line with my values?* This reflection helps you understand your feelings and ensures your response is intentional and aligned with your core beliefs.

For example, imagine your friend Mike makes a joke at your expense. You feel hurt, but after counting to ten, you pause and realize the joke hit a personal insecurity. Instead of getting defensive, you calmly explain how his comment affected you, turning the moment into a productive conversation rather than an argument.

Self-reflection isn't just useful in the moment—it also leads to long-term personal growth. By consistently pausing and thinking before reacting, you become more aware of your triggers and better equipped to handle them in the future. This practice builds emotional intelligence and resilience over time.

Incorporating counting to ten into your daily life can greatly improve your emotional regulation, especially when dealing with rudeness. It offers immediate impulse control, emotional distance, and space for reflection, helping you navigate difficult situations with more calm and composure.

Now that we've covered how to manage your emotional responses, let's explore some simple yet powerful ways to physically relax your body during moments of tension.

Physical Relaxation Methods

Dealing with rudeness can leave you feeling tense and upset, but using simple physical relaxation techniques can make a big difference. These methods help you release that tension so you can stay calm and thoughtful, rather than reacting impulsively. Let's explore a few ways to help you keep your cool and handle tough situations more effectively.

Progressive Muscle Relaxation (PMR)

Progressive Muscle Relaxation (PMR) is a great way to manage stress by focusing on the difference between tension and relaxation. It's simple: tense and then relax different muscle groups to help your body let go of built-up stress. Start by sitting comfortably or lying down, then breathe deeply—in through your nose, out through your mouth. Begin with your toes, tensing them for five seconds, then relaxing for ten to twenty seconds. Slowly work your way up through your body—calves, thighs, abdomen, chest, arms, shoulders, neck, and face—feeling the tension melt away as you go.

Studies show that PMR can effectively reduce stress and anxiety by increasing your awareness of physical tension and promoting relaxation. If you make it a regular habit, you'll have a reliable go-to strategy for staying calm when confronted with rudeness (Everything You Need to Know About Progressive Muscle Relaxation, 2022).

Stretching to Release Tension

Adding stretches to your routine is a simple but powerful way to release tension. When rudeness makes your body tighten up, stretching helps reset both your mood and muscles. For example, roll your shoulders backward for ten seconds, then forward, to ease upper back tension. Gently tip your head side to side to relieve neck strain. These small stretches signal your brain to relax and unwind.

According to research from Colorado State University, stretching reduces muscle tension and boosts mood and energy levels (Adams-Colon, 2021). By keeping your body loose, you'll find it easier to handle those frustrating situations.

Grounding Techniques for Emotional Control

When you're feeling overwhelmed, grounding techniques can help you regain control. These exercises focus on the present moment, engaging your senses and pulling you out of the emotional stress of the situation. One simple technique is the "5-4-3-2-1" exercise: name five things you can see, four things you can touch, three sounds you can hear, two scents you can smell, and one thing you can taste. Shifting your focus back to the present moment helps you stay grounded and prevents emotional overreactions.

Grounding exercises are often recommended for high-stress situations because they help break the cycle of reactive thinking and regulate emotions (Marcinek, 2024).

Body Movement to Shake Off Stress

A quick burst of physical activity, like a short walk, can instantly lift your mood and relieve stress. If you feel tense after a rude encounter, take a five-minute walk—outside or even just around the office. The fresh air and change of scenery help release endorphins, reducing stress naturally.

Research shows that short bursts of physical activity significantly lower anger and frustration (Bergland, 2022). If a walk isn't possible, even doing some quick exercises like jumping jacks or a few stretches at your desk can help you shake off stress and reset.

Combining Techniques for Greater Effect

You don't have to use these methods individually combining them can make them even more effective. Pairing deep breathing with Progressive Muscle Relaxation (PMR) can help release physical tension more efficiently. Grounding techniques can work well with stretches too, like noticing your surroundings while rolling your shoulders or stretching your neck to stay calm in stressful situations.

The other day, Greg made a snide comment during a meeting. Normally, I'd react immediately, but instead, I paused. I took a deep breath, pressed my hands on the cool table, and noticed its smooth surface under my fingers. That brief moment of stillness gave me time to roll my shoulders back, clear my mind, and respond calmly. It wasn't easy, but I felt in control and proud of how I handled it.

Another time, while working as a cashier, a customer got unnecessarily rude. Afterward, I went to the break room, sat down, and did a quick PMR session, starting from my toes and moving up to my shoulders. The tension melted away bit by bit. Then, I took a short walk around the store, feeling calmer and ready to return to work.

These small acts of self-reflection and relaxation help me stay grounded and remind me that I can choose how I react, even when things get tough.

To build emotional resilience, make these techniques part of your daily routine. Try PMR before bed, stretch in the morning, ground yourself throughout the day, and make time for movement. Over time, these habits will help you handle stress more effectively.

Finally, be kind to yourself. Rudeness often reflects the other person's struggles, not your worth. It's okay to feel upset, but remember—you control how you respond, and their behavior doesn't define you.

Reflections

How often do you use physical techniques like breathing or grounding to calm yourself, and which of these tools could you incorporate more intentionally to manage stressful or rude moments?

I've learned that combining simple techniques like progressive muscle relaxation (PMR), stretching, grounding, and even a short walk can really help manage stress. Whether it's tensing and relaxing muscles or using the "5-4-3-2-1" method to shift my focus, these tools give me more control over my emotions. Pairing them with deep breathing or a quick stretch amplifies their effects, keeping me calm even in stressful moments. This reflection reminded me that I have what I need to handle rudeness and stress with composure and resilience.

Now that we've explored how physical techniques can help you stay calm under pressure, let's dive into another powerful tool: humor. Sometimes, a well-timed laugh can defuse tension and turn a stressful moment around. In the next chapter, we'll see how humor can be your shield in handling challenging situations with ease.

5

USING HUMOR AS A SHIELD

"A good laugh is a mighty good thing, a rather too scarce a good thing."
— Herman Melville

At a family wedding in Florida during the sweltering summer, my cousin, who's never been one to filter her thoughts, glanced at me and said, "You're wearing that shirt?" For a moment, I felt the familiar sting of a snarky comment. But instead of letting it linger, I smiled and replied, "Yep, it's vintage now, I'm banking on it going up in value."

Everyone around us burst out laughing, and what could've been a tense or awkward exchange instantly became a lighthearted moment. Even my cousin, the queen of bluntness, cracked a smirk. Humor helped me deflect her rudeness without escalating the situation, and in that moment, it felt like I'd won a small victory.

That's the beauty of humor, it disarms negativity and shifts the energy of a conversation. A quick, clever comeback can turn an uncomfortable interaction into a moment of connection. In this chapter, we'll explore how finding the funny side can be one of your strongest tools when dealing with difficult people.

Finding the Funny Side

Humor not only protects your emotions but also helps lighten the mood for everyone involved. It shifts the dynamic from frustration to amusement, allowing you to handle the situation with grace. In these moments, your goal isn't to make the other person laugh, though that's always a bonus, but to shift your own mindset. By focusing on the humor of the situation, you defuse your own frustration and avoid escalating things further.

Let's say a friend shows up late for dinner and starts complaining about the traffic. Instead of feeling annoyed, you could joke, "I guess you took the scenic route today!" It's a simple, light-hearted comment that can help turn their frustration into something more manageable, while also reminding yourself not to take their grumbling personally.

Humor allows you to see the bigger picture. Life's little annoyances, whether from colleagues, customers, or even friends, are often just that: little. By using humor as a shield, you take control of your emotional response and remind yourself that sometimes, things just aren't worth getting upset about.

Humor Can Help Diffuse Tension

Humor is like a release valve when stress starts building, giving everyone a chance to breathe a little easier. It's not about making fun of the situation but finding a moment of relief. According to relief theory, humor helps us escape from stressful moments, letting us cope more effectively by calming our brains from that fight-or-flight response.

Picture a tense meeting with a looming deadline. Tossing out a light joke like, "Are we trying to beat the clock or bend it?" can get people laughing and ease the tension. Sure, the deadline is still there, but the laughter makes it feel more manageable. Humor brings the team together, offering a moment to relax and making the challenge ahead seem a little less overwhelming.

Sharing Humorous Personal Stories

Sharing personal stories that highlight the funny side of frustrating moments is a great way to handle stress. When you talk about your own experiences with rudeness or tough situations and how humor helped you cope, you become more relatable. These stories create connections because others can easily imagine themselves in your shoes.

For example, a teacher dealing with a rowdy class might share a funny story about a student's odd but innocent behavior. This not only lightens the mood but also shows the teacher's understanding of the situation. Sharing a laugh can build a stronger connection and might even help prevent future disruptions.

Similarly, a customer service rep who regularly handles difficult clients could share a funny story with colleagues about an absurd request from a customer. It gives everyone a good laugh and shows how humor can help manage even the toughest situations. Laughing together strengthens team bonds and reminds everyone that they can learn from each other's experiences.

Reframing Situations

Reframing means seeing a frustrating situation from a new perspective, making it easier to handle. When someone is rude, instead of focusing on the negativity, you can find humor in the moment.

For example, imagine being stuck in traffic after a long day. Instead of getting upset, you could reframe it as unexpected time to catch up on your favorite podcast or reflect on your day. By shifting your perspective, you turn frustration into something positive. Reframing helps you cope better and turns everyday irritations into opportunities for a laugh.

Daily Humor Practices

Building resilience through humor takes practice but can become second nature over time. A great way to start is by keeping a humor journal, jotting down funny moments or observations from your day. Looking back on these entries trains your mind to find humor even in frustrating situations.

You can also make humor a daily habit by surrounding yourself with things that make you laugh—whether it's watching a funny show, reading a good book, or chatting with a witty friend. These light moments lift your mood and help you naturally find joy in life's annoyances.

Brightening someone's day with a playful comment or witty banter also helps. It builds positivity and strengthens your ability to find humor in everyday situations. Over time, these small habits will help you become more resilient to stress and frustration.

Shifting your perspective to find humor in life's challenges makes dealing with them easier. When humor is part of your routine, even rudeness becomes an opportunity to laugh.

And sometimes, the best laughs come from poking fun at yourself. Next, we'll explore self-deprecating humor and how it helps you connect with others while keeping things light.

Self-Deprecating Humor

Self-deprecating humor can be a great way to handle rudeness and lighten the mood. By making a joke about yourself, you show others you're not taking things too seriously, which can ease tension and make conversations more relaxed. Admitting your flaws with humor can help build connections, showing that "I'm not perfect either," and making others feel more comfortable.

For example, if a colleague harshly critiques your work, you might respond with, "Guess I'll add that to the list of things my dog thinks I'm bad at!" This shows you're not overly bothered by the criticism and can laugh at yourself, which often lowers defenses and makes the situation feel less confrontational.

However, it's important to use self-deprecating humor in moderation. While it can break the ice, too much can affect your confidence over time. It's all about balance. A well-placed joke can diffuse tension but overdoing it might undermine your self-esteem.

Timing and context matter. A small joke in a high-pressure meeting can shift the mood and create a moment of connection. Just remember to gauge your audience—self-deprecation works best with people who know you well. In front of clients or higher-ups, it could come across as a lack of confidence.

When used wisely, self-deprecating humor shows humility and resilience. It helps calm tense situations, showing you can laugh at yourself without being shaken by criticism. Humor, like emotional first aid, protects your well-being and helps prevent stress from taking a toll.

While self-deprecating humor can be effective, other types—like sarcasm—are trickier to navigate. Next, we'll explore how to use humor styles like teasing and sarcasm carefully to avoid misunderstandings.

Sarcasm vs. Friendly Teasing

Understanding the difference between sarcasm and friendly teasing is key to handling rudeness well. While sarcasm often has a harsh or defensive tone, teasing is lighthearted and can build connections when used right.

Sarcasm relies on context and subtle cues, like an eye roll or smirk, to communicate a hidden, often negative message. For example, saying "Nice job" after someone drops food might seem harmless, but the tone makes it critical and can cause tension. In contrast, teasing is playful and less likely to hurt feelings. Telling a perpetually late co-worker, "Do you ever wake up on time?" with a smile softens the remark, making it easier to laugh off.

Using humor, whether sarcasm or teasing, depends on knowing your audience and the situation. Sarcasm can work with close friends who get your humor, but teasing is usually safer in professional settings. Studies show that sarcasm can be easily misunderstood, especially by older adults or in formal contexts, making teasing the better option to avoid awkwardness.

For instance, in a meeting where things don't go as planned, saying, "Looks like we all need extra coffee today!" with a smile lightens the mood without putting anyone on the spot. In contrast, a sarcastic remark like, "Well, that was enlightening," could embarrass the person and add tension.

When using humor, keep a few tips in mind:

- Know your relationship: Stick to teasing with people who know you well. Sarcasm works best with close friends who get your style.
- Consider the context: Avoid sarcasm in formal or high-stress situations like work meetings. Teasing is usually a safer bet.
- Watch your tone: Make sure your delivery matches your intent, so it doesn't come off as mean-spirited.
- Keep it positive: Your goal with humor should be to lighten the mood, not to belittle.

Mastering the balance between sarcasm and teasing can make a big difference in handling rudeness and improving your social interactions.

Humor as a Social Tool

Humor is a powerful way to improve communication, resolve conflicts, and build relationships. It lightens tense situations and promotes openness. Picture a stressful meeting: a light joke can ease the tension, helping everyone relax and share ideas more freely. Humor builds trust and encourages better communication.

One of humor's strengths is its ability to redirect tough conversations. If someone makes a rude comment, a witty but kind response can diffuse tension and show emotional intelligence. This turns a potentially negative exchange into a positive one, making challenging situations more manageable.

However, humor isn't one-size-fits-all. What makes one person laugh may offend another, especially in diverse settings. Being aware of cultural sensitivities and personal preferences is key. For example, self-deprecating humor works in some cultures but might seem like insecurity in others. Adjusting your humor to fit the situation ensures it connects in a positive way.

In the workplace, humor boosts morale and strengthens teamwork. Teams that laugh together tend to work better together. Leaders who use humor wisely build stronger connections, making themselves more approachable. However, timing and context are crucial—humor needs to be appropriate for the moment.

Humor also builds empathy and deepens connections. Sharing a funny story or lighthearted joke shows your human side, encouraging openness and trust. In stressful situations, humor can ease tension and make difficult moments easier to navigate.

When used thoughtfully, humor can reduce stress, strengthen relationships, and open doors to honest conversations. By being mindful of your audience and the situation, you can use humor to make interactions more positive and meaningful, both personally and professionally.

Reflections

How can you use humor to build connections and ease tension while still respecting boundaries, and where could you improve your awareness of timing and context in your daily interactions?

I've realized how humor enhances communication and builds stronger relationships. It's not just about making people laugh—it breaks down barriers and eases conflict resolution. I especially connected with the idea that understanding cultural sensitivities is key, particularly in diverse workplaces. Humor can make leaders more approachable, but timing and context are crucial to keeping it professional. What stood out most was how humor fosters empathy and emotional connections, making work interactions less stressful and more enjoyable without losing professionalism.

While humor helps us connect and reduce tension, empathy deepens our understanding. By stepping into someone else's shoes, we build trust and strengthen relationships. Now, let's shift from using humor to lighten situations to applying empathy to create meaningful, lasting bonds with those around us.

6

WALKING IN THEIR SHOES

"When you show deep empathy toward others, their defensive energy goes down, and positive energy replaces it. That's when you can get more creative in solving problems." — Stephen R. Covey

I was at the grocery store, rushing through the checkout line, when the cashier seemed distracted and slow. My first reaction was impatience. I had places to be. But then I noticed her tired eyes and the deep sighs between each customer. She was probably having a long day, maybe dealing with her own frustrations. Suddenly, my annoyance faded, replaced by understanding. I've had those days too.

Empathy isn't just about noticing how someone feels; it's about trying to understand why they feel that way. In that moment, I made a small decision, I smiled and said, "Long day, huh? Hang in there." Her expression softened, and for the first time during our interaction, she smiled back. It was a small exchange, but you could feel the shift. The tension dissolved, replaced by a brief, shared moment of human connection.

Covey's quote captures this perfectly. When we lead with empathy, we don't just change our perspective; we change the energy around us. What starts as an internal shift can become a ripple effect, turning moments of frustration into opportunities for connection and understanding.

Understanding Their Perspective

Seeing things from the viewpoint of someone being rude can help you feel more compassionate and less frustrated. Often, rudeness comes from personal struggles we don't know about. For example, a stressed-out cashier might snap at you because of financial problems or personal loss. When you consider these possibilities, responding kindly becomes easier.

Misunderstandings can quickly create distance, but understanding someone's perspective strengthens connections. It's easy to feel attacked and respond defensively, but their behavior usually has more to do with their own issues than with you. Taking a moment to pause before reacting helps you avoid escalating conflicts and creates space for empathy.

Everyone has a backstory that shapes their actions. For example, a co-worker who seems grumpy might be dealing with tough personal challenges. When you understand their background, it becomes easier to show compassion and bridge the gap.

By pausing and considering why someone is acting out, you can gather your thoughts and respond calmly. This small shift in perspective turns potential conflict into an opportunity for connection. It's not about justifying bad behavior but acknowledging that we don't always know what others are going through.

Misunderstandings are a common source of tension. For instance, a curt email from a colleague might seem hostile but could simply reflect their busy day. Instead of reacting negatively, seeking clarity can turn potential conflicts into moments of collaboration.

Listening to others' stories is another powerful way to build empathy. When you take the time to hear someone's struggles, it humanizes them and reduces frustration. Simple acts of listening can make a big difference in creating a culture of understanding.

Pausing before reacting helps avoid impulsive responses. Stressful encounters often trigger automatic reactions, but a brief pause to take a breath or count to ten can shift your perspective and prevent things from escalating.

Ultimately, seeing the situation from the other person's perspective allows you to navigate frustrating encounters with more grace. Empathy not only benefits others but also reduces your own stress and builds emotional resilience.

Now that we've explored how empathy can influence your reactions, let's dive into how it affects communication and strengthens relationships.

The Role of Empathy in Communication

Empathy is a powerful tool for managing rude behavior more effectively. When you understand where someone is coming from, it's easier to stay calm in frustrating situations. Strengthening your empathy helps improve your interactions, even when things get tough. Now, let's explore how empathy enhances communication and look at strategies for navigating difficult conversations.

Active Listening

Active listening is key to empathetic communication. It's more than hearing words; it's about being fully present and focused on the speaker. By maintaining eye contact, nodding, and showing engagement, you demonstrate that you care about understanding their viewpoint. For example, if a co-worker snaps at you, responding calmly with a focus on their words can help reduce tension.

Avoid interrupting or thinking about your reply while they're speaking. Simple phrases like, "I see" or "That sounds tough" show you're engaged. This kind of listening affirms their feelings and helps ease a tense situation.

Non-Violent Communication

Nonviolent communication focuses on understanding, not blame. It's about expressing your feelings and needs without attacking the other person. For example, if a client is upset about a missed deadline, instead of getting defensive, you might say, "I noticed we missed the deadline, and it's stressing me out because of the impact on our schedule. Can we talk about what happened and find a solution together?" This approach promotes collaboration and reduces tension.

Positive Body Language

Your body language says a lot. Open, positive body language—like standing tall, relaxing your posture, and making gentle eye contact—shows you're approachable. For instance, at a service counter, responding to an angry customer with a sincere smile and calm body language signals that you're there to help, not argue.

Be mindful of cultural differences, as body language can vary. Adjusting your non-verbal cues based on context improves the effectiveness of your communication.

Empathetic Responses

Empathetic responses can turn tension into understanding. Reflecting on someone's emotions, like saying, "It sounds like you're feeling overwhelmed," shows that you're listening and care. You don't have to agree with them, but acknowledging their feelings can diffuse frustration.

Using the DESC model—Describe, Express, Specify, Conclude—can help. For example, if someone interrupts you, you might say, "I felt thrown off when you interrupted earlier. Could we hold questions until the end?" This expresses your needs respectfully and encourages more thoughtful communication.

Empathy helps you connect with others and manage tough situations calmly. Next, we'll explore how to turn anger into compassion and respond to frustrations with kindness.

Turning Anger Into Compassion

Turning anger into compassion helps build deeper connections and reduce conflict. When faced with rudeness, it's natural to feel frustrated, but learning to manage those emotions can lead to more positive outcomes. Instead of feeding negativity, you can approach the situation with understanding, which benefits both the other person and your emotional well-being.

Recognizing your emotional triggers is the first step. For example, if past experiences have left you feeling undervalued, criticism might hit a nerve. By identifying the emotions behind your reactions, you can pause and respond thoughtfully rather than impulsively.

Emotional literacy, or being aware of your feelings, helps prevent outbursts and fosters better communication. For instance, if someone's rude behavior makes you feel disrespected, calmly saying, "I felt uncomfortable with your tone," is more effective than reacting with anger.

Shifting your perspective also helps. Instead of seeing a rude comment as a personal attack, consider that the other person might be going through a tough time. This mental shift allows you to react with empathy instead of frustration.

Self-compassion is equally important. When someone is rude, remind yourself that their actions reflect more on them than on you. Don't take it personally—tell yourself, "I'm doing my best, and this doesn't define me."

Gratitude is another great tool for managing anger. Focusing on what's going well, even when you're frustrated, can help you stay balanced. For instance, reflecting on supportive friends or recent successes can ease the stress of a tough moment.

One way to put this into practice is by keeping an emotion diary. Track moments of anger, identify triggers, and note how you responded. Over time, this helps you recognize patterns and handle situations more calmly.

By understanding your triggers, practicing self-compassion, and embracing gratitude, turning anger into empathy becomes second nature. Next, let's explore some empathy exercises to build on these skills.

Practical Empathy Exercises

Practicing empathy in everyday situations can make a huge difference in how you connect with others, especially during frustrating encounters. Whether it's through empathy mapping, role-playing, reflection journaling, or small acts of kindness, these simple techniques can help you better understand others' feelings and see things from their perspective.

Empathy mapping is a great way to organize someone's thoughts, feelings, words, and actions into clear categories. Let's say you're dealing with someone who seems upset—you'd break down what they might be *feeling*, *thinking*, *saying*, and *doing*. For example, they might be feeling anxious, thinking, "I'm under too much pressure," saying, "I can't handle this," and avoiding eye contact. By mapping out their emotions like this, you get a clearer sense of their mindset and can respond more thoughtfully.

Role-playing is a hands-on way to build empathy by stepping into someone else's shoes. You can act out everyday frustrating situations, like dealing with a stressed customer or resolving a conflict with a colleague. One person plays the role needing empathy, while the other listens and responds. Afterward, talk about how it felt and what you learned. Role-playing helps you understand different perspectives, making it easier to show empathy in real-life situations.

After a challenging interaction, reflection journaling helps you process your feelings. Write down what happened, how you felt, and why. Ask yourself questions like, "Why did I react this way?" or "What could have caused their behavior?" This practice helps you understand both your emotions and the emotions of others, making it easier to react with empathy in future encounters.

Simple gestures like holding the door for someone, offering a kind word, or helping with a small task are effortless ways to practice empathy. These small acts remind you to focus on others' feelings and create positive connections. When you make kindness a habit, it naturally brings more empathy into your daily life.

Incorporating these exercises into your routine helps you grow your empathy skills. Whether you're mapping out someone's feelings, role-playing different perspectives, reflecting on your reactions, or spreading kindness, you'll find it easier to connect with others and handle tough situations with understanding and compassion.

Reflections

How might approaching rude behavior with empathy change the outcome of your interactions and your own emotional state?

I connected with the idea that empathy can truly reshape how I respond to rude behavior. By understanding where the other person is coming from, I can shift my reaction and prevent situations from escalating. Active listening resonated with me as well, it's about more than just hearing; it's about being fully present and validating someone's emotions. Self-compassion helps me stay grounded during tough moments, while practicing gratitude softens the impact of stress. I also found empathy mapping to be an insightful tool, and small acts of kindness feel like simple yet powerful ways to strengthen connections with others.

Now that you understand how empathy can transform your reactions and relationships, it's time to focus on emotional resilience. Building resilience will empower you to handle stress, recover from setbacks, and maintain emotional stability in challenging situations. Let's explore key habits that can strengthen your resilience moving forward.

7

BUILDING EMOTIONAL RESILIENCE

"Resilience is accepting your new reality, even if it's less good than the one you had before. You can fight it, or you can do your best to build something better."
— Elizabeth Edwards

While stuck in traffic and barely moving, a driver behind me starts aggressively honking, as if he could magically part the sea of cars. Instead of throwing my hands up in frustration or even honking back, I took a deep breath, turned up the music, and focused on staying calm. On the inside, though, I was definitely tempted to give them a piece of my mind.

That moment reminded me that resilience isn't just about keeping your cool when things heat up. It's about accepting life's little annoyances as inevitable and choosing to respond in a way that strengthens you rather than drags you down. Sure, I couldn't control the other driver's impatience, but I could control my reaction, walking away from that moment a little more grounded and ready for whatever came next.

Edwards' words capture this perfectly. Resilience is about embracing life's imperfections and finding ways to grow from them. Each time you choose calm over chaos or let go of the urge to match someone's negativity, you're building a better, more unshakable version of yourself.

And here's the best part: resilience doesn't require grand, life-altering events. It's built in these small, everyday moments, like sitting in traffic. Let's explore how you can develop this strength step by step, no matter what challenges life throws your way.

Daily Resilience Practices

Building emotional resilience is key to handling those frustrating encounters with grace. And it doesn't have to be complicated! Simple, daily habits can make all the difference in helping you manage life's curveballs. Here are a few easy ways to strengthen your mental toughness and improve how you respond to negativity.

Morning Affirmations

Starting your day with positive affirmations can really set the tone. Simple phrases like "I'm capable" or "I handle challenges with ease" might feel small, but they can build your confidence and prepare you for whatever comes your way. It's all about feeding your mind the right thoughts before the day gets going.

To make affirmations stick:

1. Take a quiet moment each morning.
2. Stand in front of the mirror and say your affirmations out loud.
3. Yes, it might feel awkward at first, but keep at it!

Over time, these affirmations will feel more natural, and you'll start noticing a shift in your mindset. For an extra boost, jot them down and stick them where you can see them—like on your fridge or bathroom mirror. This way, they'll remind you of your inner strength whenever you face a tough situation.

Gratitude Journaling

A gratitude journal is a simple but powerful way to boost resilience. Focusing on the things you're thankful for helps you steer your thoughts away from the negative and puts you in a better mood. It's a great way to balance the stress of dealing with rude behavior.

All you need to do is set aside a few minutes each day to write down three things you're grateful for. They don't have to be big—maybe it's enjoying your morning coffee, a nice chat with a friend, or just the fact that you got through the day. Keeping it consistent is the key. Over time, you'll start to see more positivity in your life, which will help you stay grounded when things get rough.

Engaging in Physical Activity

Getting your body moving is a fantastic way to build emotional resilience. Sure, exercise is good for your physical health, but it also does wonders for your mind. Regular physical activity releases those feel-good endorphins that lift your mood and help you deal with stress. Plus, it lowers stress hormones, making it easier to handle tough situations with more clarity.

And it doesn't have to be anything intense! Whether it's a walk, yoga, dancing in your living room, or a light workout, choose something that feels fun and fits into your routine. Aim for about 30 minutes of movement most days, and you'll start noticing how much more grounded you feel—even when someone's being difficult.

The Power of Small Daily Habits

You don't have to overhaul your whole life to build resilience. These small, simple habits—morning affirmations, gratitude journaling, and regular physical activity—can really help you handle rude encounters without letting them ruin your day. With each small step, you're building a stronger foundation for your mental and emotional well-being.

Now that you've got some daily tools for resilience, let's dive into how self-care plays a role in bouncing back from life's challenges. After all, when you take care of yourself, everything else becomes a little easier to handle!

The Importance of Self-Care

Maintaining emotional resilience in the face of rudeness is essential, and self-care plays a vital role in keeping you mentally and emotionally strong. Prioritizing your well-being helps you handle negative interactions with patience and grace. Key practices like relaxation, healthy eating, sleep, and hobbies bolster your emotional resilience.

Relaxation is crucial for recharging your mind. Taking just a few minutes daily to unwind—whether through deep breathing, meditation, or quiet reflection—can make a big difference in managing tension. These moments allow you to reset, creating the mental space to handle stress and rudeness more calmly.

Healthy eating fuels both your body and mind. A balanced diet rich in lean proteins, grains, fruits, and vegetables supports emotional well-being. Omega-3s from foods like salmon and walnuts help reduce anxiety, while sugary or processed foods can trigger mood swings, making it harder to stay composed during stressful moments. Choosing nutritious options strengthens your ability to respond calmly.

Adequate sleep is often overlooked but critical. Getting at least seven hours of sleep each night restores your energy and improves your mood, making you better equipped to handle stress. Establishing a sleep routine—like winding down with a book or avoiding screens before bed—helps ensure quality rest and a more balanced mindset.

Nurturing hobbies is a great way to relieve stress. Doing activities like gardening, cooking, or painting brings joy and gives you something positive and creative to focus on. These hobbies boost your confidence and serve as a healthy distraction from everyday pressures. Plus, when you choose hobbies that involve social interaction, like joining a class or group, you also expand your support network, giving you more emotional resources when you need them.

Incorporating self-care into your daily routine strengthens your emotional resilience over time. Taking moments to relax helps you stay calm even when things get hectic. Eating healthy keeps your mood balanced, and getting enough sleep sharpens your clarity and focus.

Hobbies bring joy and balance, making it easier to maintain a positive outlook when faced with negativity.

By investing in self-care, you're building the emotional strength to face life's challenges with grace. Over time, these habits help you stay grounded and resilient, turning every encounter with rudeness into a chance to learn, grow, and strengthen your resilience.

Realizing From Each Venture

Every rude encounter, while frustrating, can actually be a valuable opportunity for emotional growth. It's easy to let negative emotions take over, but shifting your mindset can turn those tough moments into important lessons. Instead of dwelling on the hurt, you can use these experiences to gain insight into yourself and how you handle pressure. In this section, we'll dive into how simple habits like reflecting on your experiences, getting feedback from others, embracing a growth mindset, and jotting down your thoughts can help you transform challenges into powerful learning experiences.

Reflective Practices

Reflecting on rude encounters helps you learn from them and gives you a clearer picture of your emotions and reactions. When you step back and think about the interaction, it becomes easier to see it more objectively. Ask yourself, "How did their words affect me? Why did I react the way I did?" This reflection helps you understand the triggers in both your behavior and others, giving you more control next time.

Think about those specific comments from co-workers or family members that get under your skin. Reflecting on why they affect you can uncover deeper issues like insecurities or past hurts. By recognizing these patterns, you'll be better prepared to respond calmly next time. Each reflection strengthens your emotional resilience, helping you move from reacting impulsively to responding gracefully.

Seeking Feedback

Seeking feedback from people you trust is another great way to learn from rude encounters. Sometimes our emotions cloud our judgment, making it hard to see the situation clearly. A friend or colleague who offers balanced advice can give you a fresh perspective you might not have considered.

Talk to someone you trust and explain what happened. Ask them for their take on it. They might offer suggestions for alternative ways to handle things or help you better understand the rude person's behavior. Constructive feedback like this can highlight areas for growth and keep you from taking things too personally. It's a vital part of building emotional resilience, as it not only improves how you respond but also strengthens your relationships.

Adopting a Growth Mindset

Embracing Shifting your mindset to focus on growth can also help you handle rude behavior more effectively. Instead of seeing these interactions as setbacks, view them as opportunities to grow. A growth mindset means you believe you can improve through effort and learning. This perspective helps you take rude comments or negative experiences as opportunities to better understand yourself and others.

For example, if someone criticizes your work, try seeing it as a chance to assess their feedback rather than taking it personally. With a growth mindset, challenges become chances to learn and develop, rather than failures. Over time, you'll focus less on the rudeness and more on how you can grow from it.

Documenting Insights

Documenting what you've learned from these encounters reinforces those lessons. Keeping a journal of your experiences helps you track your progress and gives you a personal guide for future situations.

After each encounter, jot down what happened, how you reacted, any feedback you received, and what you learned. Over time, you'll build a collection of valuable insights that reflect your emotional growth. When faced with similar challenges, looking back on these entries will remind you of what worked in the past and keep you grounded.

Journaling can also help you spot patterns. If the same type of comment irritates you repeatedly, it might signal something deeper, like an issue with self-esteem. Documenting your growth is not only useful for personal development but can also be valuable in professional settings. When discussing growth with mentors or supervisors, having concrete examples of how you've handled tough situations shows your commitment to building resilience.

Now that you know how to turn rude encounters into learning opportunities, let's move on to building a positive daily routine. Small, consistent practices can help you manage stress and stay emotionally strong, no matter what comes your way.

Creating a Positive Daily Routine

Building a daily routine that supports emotional resilience is crucial, especially when dealing with challenges like rudeness or stress. Whether it's a co-worker with an attitude or a customer being difficult, having structured habits helps you stay grounded and respond calmly. A solid routine provides the foundation to navigate the day with grace, no matter what comes your way. Here are some strategies to help create a routine that strengthens emotional resilience.

Morning Rituals

Begin your day with purposeful activities to set a positive tone and take control. A consistent morning routine helps you prepare for anything, including rude encounters. Waking up at the same time each day creates a natural rhythm for your body, boosting your energy and mental focus from the moment you start your day.

Incorporating physical exercise is an excellent way to build resilience. Just 20 minutes of walking, yoga, or stretching can lift your mood and reduce stress. Exercise releases endorphins—the feel-good hormones that keep you calm and resilient throughout the day.

A nutritious breakfast also sets the right foundation. Foods rich in protein, fiber, and healthy fats provide lasting energy and keep you focused. Skipping breakfast or consuming too much caffeine can make you irritable and reduce your ability to handle stress. Try herbal tea if you want a calmer start instead of coffee, helping you maintain composure throughout the day.

Regular Check-Ins

Throughout the day, staying in touch with your emotions is key to managing reactions effectively. Regular check-ins help you stay aware of how you're feeling and allow you to adjust before stress takes over. A simple deep breath, a quick stretch, or a brief moment of reflection can work wonders.

Set a reminder on your phone or computer to pause and check in with yourself. Ask, "How am I feeling right now?" and adjust if needed. If you notice feelings of frustration or stress building, take a brief break to clear your head before continuing.

Journaling during these check-ins can provide clarity. Writing down your thoughts for just a few minutes helps identify patterns in your emotional responses, giving you better insight into what triggers stress and how to manage it.

Setting Intentions

Another powerful practice is setting intentions for how you want to approach your day emotionally. This shifts your mindset from reacting to situations to deciding ahead of time how you will handle challenges like rude comments or stressful interactions.

Each morning, spend a few minutes setting your emotional goals. For instance, you could aim to remain patient during tough conversations or choose kindness, even when others are rude. These intentions become mental anchors that guide you through the day.

Writing down your intentions can make them more impactful. Place them somewhere visible—on your desk or phone—to remind yourself throughout the day. Revisiting these intentions helps you stay grounded when faced with difficult moments.

Evening Reflections

Evening reflections at the end of the day, taking time for reflection helps you unwind and review how things went. Reflecting on your successes and identifying areas for improvement provides closure and a sense of accomplishment.

Find a quiet moment before bed to think about your day. Start by focusing on what went well, like managing a rude interaction with patience or handling a stressful situation with ease. Recognizing these wins boosts your confidence and reinforces positive habits.

If something didn't go as planned, view it as a learning experience rather than a failure. Reflect on how you can handle similar situations better next time, turning challenges into opportunities for growth.

Creating a Calm Bedtime Ritual

Creating a calming bedtime routine signals to your brain that it's time to wind down. Simple activities like reading, listening to music, or a skincare routine help relax your mind and body. Sticking to a regular sleep schedule ensures that you get the rest you need to face the next day's challenges with emotional stability.

Incorporating relaxation, balanced meals, and enough sleep into your routine builds your emotional resilience over time. These small, consistent practices make it easier to manage stress and rudeness while staying centered and calm, turning each day into an opportunity for growth and balance.

Reflections

What small, consistent habits could you start incorporating into your daily routine to strengthen your emotional resilience and better prepare for life's challenging moments?

Why Do Rude People Piss Me Off!

I've realized that building emotional resilience isn't just about big, dramatic changes—it's about the small, consistent habits that truly help me handle stress better. Simple things, like getting enough sleep, eating nourishing foods, and making space for relaxation, play a huge role in maintaining my emotional strength. Another thing that stood out to me is how nurturing hobbies gives me a healthy outlet, helping me stay grounded even when things get tough.

Reflecting on rude encounters also helped me spot the emotional triggers that catch me off guard. Recognizing these patterns gives me a chance to prepare and respond more thoughtfully next time. I've learned that having a positive, structured routine helps me feel emotionally stable and resilient, and I'm committed to making this a daily practice.

Pause for a Moment

If something in these pages has helped you, gave you clarity, helped you refocus, or reminded you of your strength, I want you to know this:

I didn't write this book from a tower. I wrote it in the middle of my own struggles, doubts, and desire to be better. If it's made an impact, that means everything.

But here's the truth.

This book will only reach others because of you.

Amazon uses reviews to decide who sees this. No ads. No shortcuts. Just real people sharing their voice.

Why Do Rude People Piss Me Off!

IF YOU BELIEVE in this message, if it helped you,

please take 60 seconds and leave a review.

It's not just feedback. It's fuel to keep this going, for me and for the next reader who needs it.

Scan the QR code or Click Here and be part of the story.

8

COMMUNICATION SKILLS

"The single biggest problem in communication is the illusion that it has taken place." —George Bernard Shaw

I was sharing an idea with my team when I noticed my colleague scrolling through his phone. Suddenly, my confidence wavered, and I wasn't sure if I should keep going or just stop talking altogether. Feeling frustrated, I couldn't help but ask, "Am I interrupting something important?" He looked up, caught off guard, and quickly apologized, but by then, the energy in the room had shifted, and the conversation had lost its spark.

It was a clear example of what Shaw meant by the "illusion" of communication. On the surface, it might have seemed like a conversation was happening, words were being exchanged, but without full attention and engagement, the connection broke down. This moment taught me that communication isn't just about what we say; it's about how well we listen and engage.

In today's fast-paced world, we often fall into the trap of assuming we've communicated simply because we've spoken or heard words. But true communication demands active listening, an underrated skill that ensures both parties feel heard and understood. Let's dive into how mastering this skill can transform the way we connect with others, even in the face of rudeness or distraction.

The Art of Active Listening

Listening goes beyond just hearing someone speak; it's about really connecting with them. When you truly listen, you show that their words matter, which can defuse tension and strengthen your relationships. Tuning into vocal cues—like tone, pitch, and pace—helps you catch how someone's feeling. For example, a higher pitch might mean they're excited, while a calm tone suggests they're feeling more relaxed.

It's not just about picking up on those changes but understanding what's behind them. If a colleague's voice gets sharp, they might be frustrated. Acknowledging the emotion behind their words often leads to deeper, more meaningful conversations.

Asking simple clarifying questions like, "Can you explain what you mean?" shows you're engaged and care about getting things right. Reflecting what they've said back to them, like, "So, you're feeling a little overwhelmed by the project deadline?" makes sure you've got the message and builds trust.

Empathetic listening goes even further. It's not just about hearing their words but connecting with how they're feeling. Saying something like, "It sounds like this has been tough for you," helps the person feel understood and supported.

Non-verbal cues, like a smile or a nod, matter just as much. These little gestures show you're present and paying attention. Putting distractions aside, like your phone, helps create real, meaningful connections in every conversation.

Non-Verbal Communication Cues

Non-verbal cues play a huge role in communication, often speaking louder than words. Whether it's body language, eye contact, facial expressions, or personal space, these signals send powerful messages that help us connect with others.

For example, standing tall with open posture shows confidence and engagement, while crossed arms or avoiding eye contact can signal discomfort or defensiveness. A simple smile can break the ice, and maintaining balanced eye contact shows attentiveness without overwhelming the other person.

Personal space is also important, as some people prefer more distance in conversations. By tuning into these non-verbal cues and using them thoughtfully, you can make others feel more at ease, even when words aren't enough. These small, subtle signals can greatly enhance your communication skills and help you build stronger connections.

Body Language Awareness

Understanding how your body language, such as gestures, posture, and small shifts in stance, influences the conversation is vital to effective communication. Standing tall or sitting up straight with an open posture shows confidence and engagement. At the same time, slouching can signal disinterest or fatigue. A simple nod communicates agreement or understanding, whereas crossing your arms may make you seem defensive or uncomfortable.

If you want to become more aware of your body language, there are a few practical steps you can take:

- **Observe others:** Notice how people around you use their posture and gestures to communicate, especially in professional settings. By paying attention to others, you'll recognize common patterns that signal confidence, agreement, or discomfort.
- **Reflect on yourself:** Consider how your body language comes across. Are you showing that you're engaged and open to the conversation, or does your posture suggest you're uninterested?
- **Practice adjustments:** Maintaining an open posture, using

intentional gestures, and controlling nervous fidgeting can significantly impact how others see you.

Becoming more attuned to both your body language and that of others can help you navigate conversations more smoothly, allowing you to project the image you intend.

Eye Contact

Eye contact plays a key role in non-verbal communication, showing respect and attentiveness. It creates a connection between people and signals that you're fully engaged. Too little eye contact might make you seem distracted, while too much can feel intense or aggressive. Finding that sweet spot helps build trust and connection.

Here's how you can maintain good eye contact:

- **Use natural glances**: Try to make natural eye contact by glancing instead of staring. Briefly breaking and then returning to eye contact keeps things comfortable for both of you.
- **Be mindful of cultural differences**: Eye contact norms vary. In some cultures, too much direct eye contact can come across as disrespectful or aggressive.
- **Adjust to the context**: In casual settings, a more relaxed approach works. But in professional situations, steady eye contact can show confidence and focus.

Mastering eye contact makes others feel valued and respected, which is key to good communication.

Facial Expressions

Facial expressions are powerful in communication, expressing emotions without a word. A simple smile can make someone feel welcome, while a frown might signal concern or confusion.

Here's how to use facial expressions more effectively:

- **Smile genuinely**: A real smile sets a positive tone and makes others feel comfortable.
- **Align your expressions with your words**: If you say something positive but your face shows discomfort, it can confuse people. Make sure your expressions match what you're saying.
- **Watch for micro-expressions**: These tiny, quick facial changes can reveal how someone is feeling. Picking up on them helps you better understand their emotions.

Being aware of your own and others' facial expressions helps you connect emotionally and communicate more clearly.

Proximity and Personal Space

How close or far you stand from someone can affect how comfortable they feel during a conversation. Personal space is different for everyone and varies across cultures, so it's important to be aware of these boundaries.

Here's how to manage personal space effectively:

- **Respect boundaries**: If someone steps back or looks uncomfortable, give them space. People often use body language to signal discomfort.
- **Context matters**: In professional settings, keeping a respectful distance is usually a good idea. In social situations, how close you stand depends on the relationship and context.
- **Be aware of cultural norms**: Personal space varies across cultures. Being mindful of this helps prevent discomfort and shows respect for others' boundaries.

Paying attention to personal space creates a sense of respect and consideration in your interactions.

Integrating Non-Verbal Signals

Effectively using and reading non-verbal signals can elevate your communication. By being mindful of body language, maintaining natural eye contact, using facial expressions that match your words, and respecting personal space, you can communicate more confidently and effectively.

Here's how you can incorporate these skills into your daily life:

- **Practice in everyday situations**: Try out these techniques in casual conversations. The more you use them, the more natural they'll feel.
- **Get feedback**: Ask friends or colleagues for feedback on your non-verbal communication. They can offer valuable insights into how others perceive you.
- **Keep improving**: Communication is always evolving, so stay curious and continue learning about non-verbal cues.

Now that you're more aware of non-verbal signals, the next step is learning to respond assertively. Let's dive into how you can clearly and confidently express your thoughts and boundaries in any conversation.

Crafting Assertive Responses

Being assertive in your conversations helps build stronger relationships and keeps communication respectful, even when things get tricky. By honing this skill, you can turn difficult discussions into more productive and positive exchanges.

Using "I" Statements

"I" statements is a great way to express how you feel without making the other person feel attacked. Instead of sounding accusatory, you share your perspective. For example, saying, "I feel frustrated when meetings go overtime because it affects my schedule," focuses on your feelings rather than blaming someone else. Compare that to, "You always make meetings run late," which could easily trigger defensiveness.

"I" statements make people feel heard rather than criticized. This approach fosters understanding and shows respect for both sides, making it easier for others to see your point of view. Over time, you'll notice how this small shift can lead to more open and constructive conversations.

Staying Calm and Collected

Keeping your cool during difficult conversations is key. It's easy to let emotions take over, but that often leads to misunderstandings. Staying calm allows you to express yourself more clearly and thoughtfully.

A great way to stay composed is by practicing deep breathing. When emotions rise, taking a few deep breaths gives you a moment to collect your thoughts before responding. Another helpful trick is to stay grounded by focusing on something around you—like the feeling of your feet on the ground or the air in the room.

If you know a tough conversation is coming, mentally rehearsing it beforehand can make a huge difference. Preparing gives you the confidence to handle it without getting flustered. Staying calm shows maturity and self-control, which usually sets the tone for a more respectful and productive discussion

Setting Clear Boundaries

Clear boundaries are essential for building respectful relationships and good communication. They let people know what you need and what's okay, which helps prevent misunderstandings. Be clear and kind when setting boundaries. For example, you might say, "I need to finish this project by 5 PM, so I can't take on anything else today." This makes your needs clear without sounding confrontational.

It's also important to stick to your boundaries, even if it feels uncomfortable. Doing so shows that your limits matter and deserve respect. And remember, respecting other people's boundaries is just as important. When you honor their limits, it creates an environment of mutual respect and understanding.

Practicing the Pause

Sometimes, the best thing you can do in a tense conversation is take a pause before you respond. Reacting too quickly when emotions are high can lead to things being said that we don't really mean. Pausing gives you the chance to gather your thoughts and respond more thoughtfully.

A pause also shows the other person that you're listening. This simple gesture can change the whole dynamic of the conversation. When people feel like they're being heard, they're more likely to listen in return, making the conversation more productive.

In tough situations, a well-timed pause can also help defuse tension. Giving both sides a moment to cool down can prevent things from escalating. Practicing the pause regularly can help you stay calm and in control, even when emotions run high.

By using "I" statements, staying calm, setting clear boundaries, and practicing the pause, you can handle conversations in a more assertive and thoughtful way. This leads to better communication, stronger relationships, and more respectful interactions.

And what if the conversation starts getting heated? That's where de-escalation techniques come in handy. Knowing how to cool things down can help you steer the conversation back to a more productive place. Let's dive into those strategies next.

De-Escalation Strategies

When conversations get tense, emotions can flare, and things can go south quickly. It's easy for misunderstandings or feelings of being unheard to turn into frustration. But with a few helpful techniques, you can keep things from escalating and guide the conversation back to a calmer place.

Acknowledging Emotions

One of the most important steps is acknowledging the emotions in the room—both yours and the other person's. If someone's rudeness makes you feel disrespected, take a moment to recognize that feeling. Instead of reacting on impulse, you can stay in control and respond more thoughtfully.

Letting the other person know how you feel can also defuse the situation. Using "I" statements like, "I feel upset when our conversations get heated," can help without making them defensive. You're sharing your experience, not pointing fingers.

It's also essential to recognize the other person's emotions. Sometimes, just saying, "I understand you're frustrated," can make a big difference. When people feel heard, they often calm down because they know you're trying to see things from their perspective.

Using Humor to Diffuse Tension

Humor is a great way to lighten the mood, but timing is everything. A lighthearted joke can break the tension and help everyone take a breath, but you have to be careful. If someone's really upset, the wrong joke could make things worse.

For example, if a co-worker is venting about a stressful project, you could say something like, "Looks like we might need superhero powers for this one!" It's playful but acknowledges the frustration. But always be mindful—if humor doesn't seem to land well, it's okay to switch gears. Sometimes, humor isn't the right tool, and that's perfectly fine.

Finding Common Ground

Another way to bring down the heat is by focusing on what you and the other person have in common. Finding shared goals or mutual interests can redirect the conversation away from conflict and toward collaboration.

If a client is upset about a project delay, for instance, you could say, "We both want this project to be a success, so let's figure out the next steps together." When you focus on what you both want, it's easier to move past the tension and work toward a solution.

Suggesting a Break

Sometimes, the best thing to do in a heated situation is to hit pause. Suggesting a break gives everyone time to cool off and gather their thoughts. This can keep things from escalating and give both sides a chance to reflect.

You might say, "I think a short break would help us both cool down and come back with clear heads." Just be sure to set a time to pick things back up, so it doesn't feel like you're avoiding the issue. A structured break can make all the difference, allowing everyone to return with a fresh perspective.

Giving the other person space to process can be incredibly helpful. Don't rush it, pushing to resolve things too quickly can make things worse. A little patience can go a long way.

Reflections

How can improving your listening skills and communication habits help you stay calm and foster respect, even when faced with rudeness?

I've come to see how much rudeness can throw off effective communication, especially when distractions like phones get in the way. This made me realize just how important active listening is for building solid connections and avoiding misunderstandings.

Reflective and empathetic listening stood out because they help me ensure I truly understand the speaker's message while also building trust in the conversation. I also learned that non-verbal cues, like eye contact and body language, are just as powerful as spoken words. Assertiveness, especially using "I" statements, along with taking a break during heated moments, can really help keep things calm and respectful when dealing with difficult people.

Now that you've strengthened your communication skills and learned how to handle rude interactions, it's time to focus on something just as important: letting go. Whether it's moving past frustration or releasing resentment, mastering the art of letting go can transform how you navigate difficult situations gracefully and effortlessly.

9

MASTERING THE ART OF LETTING GO

"Forgiveness is letting go of the hope that the past can be changed."
— Oprah Winfrey

I used to get so frustrated when my neighbor's little dogs barked nonstop. One day, after an especially noisy stretch, I stared out the window, mentally drafting a complaint. But then I paused and asked myself, "What am I gaining from this?" The more I clung to my irritation, the worse I felt. So, I made a choice: let it go. Instantly, it felt like a weight had lifted, and my mood brightened. I found myself less reactive to the barking, and my focus shifted to enjoying my day.

Oprah's words ring true in moments like these. Whether it's barking dogs or bigger life frustrations, we often hold onto the hope that something, or someone, will change to suit our expectations. But the real freedom comes when we release that hope and focus on what we can control: our response. Letting go is just the beginning. Now, let's explore how practicing forgiveness can take that freedom to an even deeper level.

Practicing Forgiveness

Forgiveness frees you from resentment and emotional pain. When someone treats you rudely, it's natural to feel hurt, but holding onto anger only weighs you down. Forgiving isn't about excusing bad behavior, it's about healing yourself. Letting go of anger creates space for peace and clarity.

A helpful way to start is by writing a forgiveness letter, even if you don't send it. This process lets you express your feelings, acknowledge the hurt, and move forward. It's a powerful tool to help release negative emotions and find closure.

Self-forgiveness is just as important. We're often our harshest critics, but learning to forgive yourself is key to emotional well-being. Mistakes are part of being human, and forgiving yourself allows for growth without being trapped by guilt. When self-blame creeps in, pause and ask whether you're being too harsh. Be kind to yourself, and focus on what you need to move forward.

Taking action also helps with self-forgiveness. Apologize if needed, make amends, and take steps to avoid repeating the mistake. Forgiving yourself takes time, so be patient with the process. Each step forward brings you closer to healing.

Forgiveness isn't a one-time event, it's an ongoing practice. If old feelings resurface, revisit them with compassion. Over time, this practice strengthens your emotional resilience and helps you stay grounded.

Holding onto resentment can harm your health, raising stress levels and affecting your well-being. Forgiving releases this burden, lowering stress and boosting your mental and physical health.

Ultimately, forgiveness empowers you. It frees you from the past and opens the door to a more peaceful, joyful life. Now that you've explored the power of forgiveness, let's dive into managing stress effectively to stay balanced, even in tough situations.

Stress-Relief Techniques

Rude encounters can quickly overwhelm you, but managing stress is essential for staying positive. By handling stress effectively, you can prevent negativity from spoiling your day.

Movement as a Tension Reliever

Exercise is a great way to release anxiety after stressful situations. Whether it's jogging, hitting the gym, or a brisk 20-minute walk, movement triggers endorphins—those "feel-good" hormones that lift your mood and clear your mind. With a quick boost, you'll be better equipped to stay calm during rude encounters.

Channeling Stress Through Hobbies

Hobbies are a fantastic way to release built-up tension. Whether it's painting, writing, or crafting, creative activities allow you to express negative emotions in a positive way. Focusing on something enjoyable helps you shift your mind away from stress and leaves you feeling more accomplished and relaxed.

The Power of a Support System

Leaning into your support system by talking to a friend or family member after dealing with rudeness can make a big difference. Venting your frustrations to someone who listens and cares can help you feel validated and supported, making the rude encounter seem less significant.

Taking Breaks to Reset

Short breaks throughout the day help you reset after stressful encounters. Whether it's taking a few deep breaths or stepping outside for a walk, these breaks give your mind time to calm down so you can approach situations with more clarity

Practicing Assertiveness

Being assertive is key to handling rude behavior calmly. By standing up for yourself respectfully, you set boundaries and prevent negativity from affecting you. A firm, calm response, like "I don't appreciate that", can help keep the situation in check without escalating tension.

Engaging in Joyful Activities

Balance negativity by focusing on things that bring you joy. Whether it's spending time with friends or engaging in a favorite hobby, these activities remind you that one rude moment doesn't define your day. Self-care routines like getting enough sleep and staying hydrated also help build resilience.

Now that you've got strategies for handling stress, let's dive into setting personal boundaries—critical for preventing stress from rude encounters in the first place.

Focusing on Personal Boundaries

Setting and maintaining personal boundaries is crucial for managing rudeness and negativity. Clear limits protect you from the emotional effects of disrespectful behavior. Start by identifying what triggers you, such as interruptions or certain comments. Once you know your boundaries, communicate them directly and confidently. For example, say, "Interrupting me feels disrespectful. Please let me finish speaking." This assertive but calm approach sets the expectation for respectful treatment.

It's important to consistently reinforce your boundaries. If someone oversteps, politely remind them, like saying, "I'd like to finish before you respond." Repeating this helps others understand how to treat you with respect and reduces frustration.

Boundaries also protect your emotional well-being. When others respect them, you feel valued, boosting your self-esteem. While setting boundaries may seem uncomfortable at first, it gets easier with practice. Over time, clear communication prevents misunderstandings and fosters healthier relationships.

The emotional benefits are significant: boundaries strengthen your self-respect, create a sense of security, and empower you to handle stress without feeling overwhelmed. You maintain control in your interactions and set the tone for more positive connections. Consistently upholding boundaries reduces stress, helping you navigate difficult situations with ease.

Now that we've covered the importance of boundaries, the next step is learning to let go of grudges. Holding onto anger or resentment weighs you down emotionally—letting go restores peace and frees up mental space for growth.

Letting Go of Grudges

Letting go of grudges isn't just about forgiving others, it's about freeing yourself from the negativity that weighs you down. Holding onto resentment drains your energy and keeps you stuck in the past, replaying old arguments that only make you feel worse. By practicing forgiveness, you allow yourself to let go and focus on what truly matters, your own peace of mind. It doesn't happen overnight, but taking small steps like acknowledging your feelings, journaling, talking to a friend, or setting boundaries can help you move forward and create space for positivity and healing. It's not about excusing the hurt, it's about choosing to free yourself from it.

How Grudges Drain Your Energy

Holding onto a grudge is like carrying a heavy emotional backpack filled with resentment, anger, and bitterness. It weighs you down, leaving you feeling drained, both mentally and physically. Every time you replay an old argument or offense in your mind, it exhausts you, making it hard to enjoy the present. Grudges keep you stuck in the past, affecting your mood, your judgment, and even how you interact with others. You might find yourself getting defensive or snapping at someone without even realizing it. Acknowledging just how much energy these grudges take from you is the first step toward letting go and creating space for a more peaceful mindset.

Emotional Detachment as a Tool

Emotional detachment is about handling your emotions without shutting them down or becoming numb. It's a way to keep your feelings in check without letting them overwhelm you. Instead of letting anger or hurt take over, you take a step back, observe what you're feeling, and choose how to react. For example, if a coworker makes a rude comment, your first instinct might be to snap back. But with emotional detachment, you pause, acknowledge your frustration, and decide not to let it ruin your mood. Over time, this helps you stay cool in difficult situations and prevents others from controlling your emotions.

Reframing Negative Experiences

Reframing negative experiences is about shifting your perspective and finding personal growth in tough situations. It's easy to feel like a victim when things go wrong, but changing how you view these moments can help you uncover valuable lessons. For instance, if a customer is rude at work, instead of focusing on their behavior, think about what you can learn—maybe it's a chance to improve your communication skills or practice patience. This shift turns a frustrating experience into an opportunity to grow. Reframing also helps you build empathy. If a friend lets you down, take a moment to consider what they might be going through before jumping to conclusions. Understanding their situation can help you let go of resentment and strengthen your relationship.

Prioritizing Personal Peace

To truly find happiness, you need to consciously prioritize your peace. This means letting go of grudges that keep you trapped in cycles of anger and resentment. Ask yourself, when faced with a grudge-worthy situation, does holding onto that negative feeling actually help you? More often than not, it only leaves you feeling stuck and upset.

To maintain your peace, it's essential to take proactive steps. Spend time with people who uplift you, do activities that bring you joy, or take a walk to clear your head. These small actions remind you that life is much bigger than the grievances you're holding onto. Another key part of protecting your peace is setting boundaries. Make sure you clearly communicate your limits to others so you can prevent future misunderstandings and preserve your emotional well-being.

Talking about your feelings can also be incredibly freeing. Whether you vent to a supportive friend or jot down your thoughts, expressing what's bothering you offers much-needed relief. In some situations, directly addressing the person involved can bring closure, allowing you to finally release that lingering anger.

Practical Steps for Letting Go of Grudges

- **Acknowledge your feelings:** Don't ignore your emotions. Permit yourself to feel upset, angry, or disappointed. Acknowledging these feelings is the first step to letting go of them.
- **Contemplate the influence:** Holding a grudge negatively impacts your mental and physical health. Understanding its negative impact can encourage you to release it.
- **Engage in actions that satisfy you:** Focus on activities that make you happy, like being with valued people, pursuing recreation, or appreciating nature. These activities help you redirect your attention away from past grievances.
- **Seek help:** Speaking to a counselor or being part of a support group can give you new tools to release long-held grudges and offer valuable outside perspectives.
- **Set boundaries:** Communicate acceptable behavior to others. Setting boundaries preserves your peace and helps prevent future grudges.

Letting go of grudges doesn't mean you're excusing lousy behavior; it means freeing yourself from the negativity that holds you back. Following these steps, you focus on your well-being and move forward with a lighter, more peaceful heart.

Reflections

How can forgiving others and setting clear boundaries create more space for joy and peace in your life?

I've come to understand just how powerful forgiveness is for healing emotional pain and finding clarity. It has shown me the importance of setting personal boundaries to protect my well-being. I've also learned that assertive communication reinforces those boundaries, encouraging others to interact with me respectfully. Practicing emotional detachment has given me the ability to stay composed, even in difficult moments. Reframing negativity helps me grow, allowing me to approach situations with more empathy. Now, I realize that prioritizing my peace is about focusing on joy and setting limits that honor my needs. Letting go of grudges is a process of acknowledging my emotions, reflecting on their impact, and seeking support when necessary.

Now that you've embraced forgiveness and boundaries, it's time to focus on something even more uplifting. By practicing positive thinking, you can approach rude situations with a fresh perspective, turning negativity into a chance for growth and peace. Let's continue to the next chapter and explore how this shift in mindset can transform your outlook on life.

10

THE POWER OF POSITIVE THINKING

"Positive thinking is more than just a tagline. It changes the way we behave. And I firmly believe that when I am positive, it not only makes me better, but it also makes those around me better." — Harvey Mackay

I used to think positive thinking was just cheesy advice, I decided to give it a shot. When the barista forgot my coffee, I smiled instead of sighing. When my leader handed me a last-minute assignment, I said, "No problem" and focused on getting it done. Even sitting in traffic became "the perfect podcast opportunity." By the end of the day, I noticed something. Sure, the circumstances didn't change, my coffee was still late, and the work was still rushed, but my mood didn't tank. That's a win, right?

Harvey Mackay's words made me think. Maybe my shift in attitude didn't just help me. The barista seemed less flustered after my smile, and my boss appeared relieved when I didn't complain. Positivity doesn't just lighten your load; it can lift the people around you too.

But here's the thing. Positivity alone isn't a magic fix for everything. That's where daily affirmations come in. They're like mental boosters, helping to reinforce that positive outlook even when the day throws curveballs. Let's break down how they can make a real difference.

Daily Affirmations

Daily affirmations are a simple way to shift your mindset toward positivity. These positive statements help you break free from negative thought patterns and develop a more constructive outlook. By repeating affirmations like "I handle difficult situations well," you gradually replace self-doubt with confidence. Over time, your brain gets trained to think more positively, almost by default.

Affirmations work by creating new neural pathways in your brain. The more you repeat them, the stronger these connections become, making positivity a natural part of your thinking. This can be incredibly helpful in tough situations, like dealing with rudeness. For instance, saying "I stay calm and composed in every situation" regularly can lower your emotional response, helping you stay cool and collected when things get heated.

Incorporating affirmations into your routine makes navigating challenges with a calm, confident attitude more natural.

Creating Effective Affirmations

To make affirmations truly effective, it's important to tailor them to your personal experiences and emotional triggers. General affirmations often lack the depth needed for lasting change. The key is identifying what causes your negative reactions—is it a certain behavior, a specific remark, or maybe a recurring situation at a particular time of day?

Once you pinpoint your triggers, create affirmations that address them directly. For instance, if you often feel undervalued at work, saying, "My contributions are valuable and appreciated" can help challenge that belief. Or, if client feedback shakes your confidence, try something like, "I am skilled and knowledgeable in my field." These personalized affirmations feel more genuine and impactful, helping to reshape your internal dialogue.

Research shows that personalization makes a big difference. A study revealed that affirmations connected to personal experiences activate brain areas linked to positive self-processing (Cascio et al., 2016). By creating affirmations that speak to your unique challenges, you're more likely to engage with them and notice meaningful changes in how you respond emotionally.

Incorporating Affirmations in Daily Life

Incorporating affirmations into your daily routine is all about consistency and creativity. Start each morning by reciting your affirmations to set a positive tone for the day. You can write them on sticky notes and place them in visible spots like your bathroom mirror, computer screen, or even on your car dashboard to remind yourself throughout the day. These small reminders help keep you on track.

If you're into tech, try using reminder apps that send your affirmations at key times during the day. Some people even record themselves saying their affirmations and play them when they need a little boost. Hearing your voice reinforce those positive thoughts can be a great way to lift your mood.

You can also weave affirmations into your existing routines. Try repeating them while having your morning coffee, during your commute, or right before bed. That way, they blend into your day naturally and don't feel forced. The key is consistency—the more you practice, the more affirmations influence your mindset and emotional responses.

Studies show that regularly using affirmations can improve self-esteem and reduce stress. Research suggests that self-affirmations can protect you from the effects of stress and even enhance problem-solving under pressure (Creswell et al., 2013). With consistent practice, affirmations help you tackle tough situations with more calm and confidence.

Measuring Progress

Tracking your progress with affirmations keeps you motivated and helps you adjust as needed. A great way to do this is by journaling. You can jot down how often you use affirmations, the situations where they help, and how they impact your emotions. Over time, you'll see patterns emerge. Maybe affirmations help you stay calm with that tricky colleague, but you notice they don't work as well when you're dealing with client feedback. This insight can guide you to tweak your affirmations to suit different challenges.

As you journal, reflect on the day's events. Did you face rudeness? How did you respond this time compared to previous situations? Did you notice any shifts in your emotional reactions? Tracking these moments helps you see your growth and refine your affirmations to make them even more effective.

You can also set up weekly or monthly check-ins to review your progress. Flip through your journal and celebrate those small wins—like staying composed in a tense conversation or bouncing back quicker after a tough day. These moments remind you that your affirmations are working and encourage you to stick with them.

Building resilience against negativity takes time, but consistent affirmation practice can make a big difference. Soon, you'll find it easier to navigate challenging situations and feel more emotionally balanced. Not only will your interactions improve, but you'll also maintain a positive outlook across all areas of life.

Now that you've seen how affirmations reshape your mindset, let's dive into another powerful tool: visualization. Like affirmations, visualization helps you build new mental pathways, but this time, you'll focus on vivid mental images instead of words. Together, these techniques can significantly strengthen your emotional resilience and help you manage stress more effectively. Let's explore how visualization can transform your approach to challenges and boost your well-being.

Visualization Techniques

Visualization isn't just about escaping reality, it's a powerful way to transform how you handle tough situations, especially when dealing with rude behavior. By imagining positive outcomes, you're creating a mental game plan for staying calm and confident in real life. This helps reduce the stress that usually comes with those frustrating encounters.

Visualization works by clearly picturing the outcome you want. Instead of daydreaming, you're actively creating a scenario where you handle challenges with grace and ease. Your brain treats these imagined situations as if they were real, making positive responses feel more natural. According to *Psychology Today*, visualization can reshape your emotions by changing brain pathways (Rhodes, 2024). The more you practice these positive responses, the more automatic they become in real-life scenarios.

To practice visualization effectively:

1. Find a quiet moment in your day where you won't be interrupted.
2. Sit comfortably, close your eyes, and take a few deep breaths to relax.
3. Think about a recent situation where someone was rude to you.
4. Instead of focusing on the negativity, imagine yourself staying calm and in control.
5. Visualize yourself responding calmly, controlling your emotions, and handling the situation with poise.
6. Now, picture the other person reacting more kindly to your calm approach.

The more you practice this, the more it'll help you stay composed when similar situations come up in real life.

Take my friend Sarah, for example. As a customer service rep, she faced irritable clients daily, leaving her drained. After starting a routine of visualization, imagining herself calmly handling these tough situations, her real-life interactions improved. Sarah's emotional resilience grew, and even her most demanding clients responded better to her calm energy. Visualization helps you create a mental blueprint for staying composed, especially when paired with affirmations like "I stay calm under pressure."

To enhance this practice, combine it with deep breathing or stretching. These simple techniques lower stress, helping you stay centered during tense moments. Research shows that deep breathing can reduce cortisol levels, decreasing anxiety and boosting your ability to stay calm. Visualizing a positive outcome while physically relaxing strengthens your emotional control and helps you manage stress effectively.

Though results won't come overnight, regular practice can help you handle negativity more effectively. Sarah's experience shows that visualization isn't just for managing rude behavior but can be used in any area of life that involves emotional stress. Like physical exercise, visualization strengthens your emotional "muscles," giving you greater control over your responses.

Now that we've covered how visualization can reshape your mindset, let's move on to another essential factor, your environment. A positive mindset thrives in a positive environment, from the people you surround yourself with to the spaces you inhabit. Let's explore how creating the right atmosphere can support your emotional well-being.

Surrounding Yourself With Positivity

A positive environment acts as a buffer against stress and negativity. Think about working in a high-pressure space for hours, it's like carrying around a weight that drags you down. On the other hand, being surrounded by uplifting people or calming spaces can help you recharge and build emotional resilience. It's like having a mental cushion that softens life's daily bumps. Studies show this too. Research highlights that positive emotions enhance resilience, making it easier to handle challenges (Meneghel et al., 2014). Like a well-tuned car rides smoothly over rough roads, a positive environment helps you tackle life's difficulties with more ease.

Finding Positivity in People and Spaces

Identifying sources of positivity is key to maintaining a strong mindset. Start by considering the people around you. Who lifts your spirits and supports you when you need it most? Friends or coworkers who listen without judgment and offer constructive feedback make a difference. They celebrate your wins and make you feel valued.

Your physical environment is just as important. Think about the places where you feel most relaxed—whether it's a peaceful park, a cozy café, or the comfort of your own home. Research from the University of Exeter suggests that even short visits to green spaces can boost mental health (Green Spaces May Boost Wellbeing for City Dwellers, 2013). Including these positive spaces in your daily routine helps you stay grounded and energized.

Building a Positive Network

Start by focusing on the relationships you already have. Strengthen these connections by checking in regularly, showing appreciation, and offering help when needed. Small gestures, like sending a quick "thank you" or being a good listener, can go a long way in reinforcing your bonds. If you're looking to expand your social circle, consider joining activities that align with your interests, whether it's a book club, exercise class, or volunteer group. Connecting with people who share your values and hobbies can help create meaningful relationships.

At work, you can foster positivity by recognizing a colleague's contributions or organizing team-building activities. A Gallup study found that teams with strong engagement and positive environments saw a 21% increase in productivity (Stone, 2023). Positivity spreads quickly, and when you share it, everyone benefits.

Shaping Your Physical Space

The spaces you live in directly impact your mood. A messy, disorganized room can increase stress, while a tidy, personalized space brings a sense of calm and control. An article from *Very Well Mind* highlights that clutter can make you feel more anxious, but keeping things organized helps you relax (Fuller, 2023). Start by clearing out any clutter, then add items that make you happy, like plants, photos, or artwork. Studies show that houseplants can reduce stress and improve your mood (Lee et al., 2015). Even at work, simple personal touches like family pictures or a cozy blanket can lift your spirits.

Lighting plays a big role in creating a positive atmosphere. Natural light boosts your mood and productivity, so try to soak up as much as you can. When that's not an option, go for warm, soft lighting to give your space a cozy vibe. You can even add a scented candle or essential oil diffuser to make your space more relaxing.

Creating Positivity Through Actions

Positivity isn't just about the space around you; it's also about how you engage with others. Regularly expressing gratitude has a ripple effect, brightening not only your day but also those around you. Whether it's a simple thank you in a personal setting or acknowledging a colleague's effort at work, these small acts of appreciation foster a more positive atmosphere. Open communication and empathy build trust and respect, helping create a supportive environment where everyone feels valued.

Setting boundaries is just as important for maintaining positivity. It's okay to step away from people, habits, or situations that drain your energy. By surrounding yourself with positive influences and clearly communicating your limits, you protect your emotional well-being and create space to grow and thrive.

Building Resilience Through Positivity

Creating a positive environment strengthens your resilience, helping you bounce back from challenges more quickly. When you surround yourself with positivity, everyday obstacles feel less overwhelming, and you're better equipped to handle whatever comes your way. It's like giving your mental and emotional health a boost, making setbacks easier to manage.

Keeping a positive environment requires ongoing effort. Take time to reflect on your surroundings and relationships, ensuring they support your well-being. This self-awareness allows you to make conscious choices about what brings positivity into your life, helping you stay grounded.

As you focus on cultivating a positive atmosphere, practices like gratitude naturally come into play. Gratitude can significantly enhance emotional resilience and brighten your outlook on life. Let's explore how fostering gratitude can deepen your relationships and bring more happiness into your daily life.

Impact of Gratitude Practices

Gratitude can help shift your focus from daily frustrations to the joys in life. By regularly recognizing and appreciating the small and big moments, you cultivate a more positive perspective. Practicing gratitude consistently can increase happiness, boost emotional resilience, and reduce stress and depression.

Starting a gratitude journal is an easy way to build this habit. Each day, jot down a few things you're thankful for, like a good cup of coffee or a thoughtful message from a friend. Over time, this helps you focus more on the positives and develop a more optimistic mindset. Research even suggests that consistent gratitude can rewire your brain, improving your emotional well-being and even your sleep.

Expressing gratitude directly to others strengthens your connections and boosts your sense of belonging. Something as simple as a thank-you note or compliment can make a big difference in your relationships. People who frequently express gratitude tend to feel more satisfied with their social interactions and overall happiness.

Gratitude isn't just for individuals, it can have a significant impact in group settings, too. In the workplace, recognizing and appreciating colleagues' efforts has been linked to higher job satisfaction and team morale. Acknowledging others creates a more supportive and positive environment for everyone.

Finally, reframing frustrating moments into gratitude helps build resilience. Instead of letting negative encounters weigh you down, try seeing them as opportunities for growth. This shift helps lessen the emotional toll of tough situations and fosters a more positive mindset.

The key is consistency. The more you practice gratitude, whether through journaling, expressing thanks, or simply noticing life's little joys, the more natural it becomes. The benefits? Better emotional health, stronger relationships, improved sleep, and a brighter outlook on life.

Reflections

How can focusing on positivity and gratitude help you reframe your challenges and create a more empowering outlook on life?

In this chapter, I realized that while positive thinking doesn't solve everything, it helps keep small problems from ruining my day. Daily affirmations offer a simple way to shift my mindset, helping me replace negative thoughts with more empowering ones. I also learned that personalizing these affirmations makes them even more impactful, especially when dealing with emotional triggers. Adding visualization techniques has boosted my confidence in handling tough situations. Surrounding myself with positive people and practicing gratitude daily have strengthened my emotional resilience and overall well-being.

Now that you've embraced positivity and gratitude, the next step is setting healthy boundaries. The upcoming chapter will show you how boundaries aren't about shutting people out but about protecting your peace and energy. When you set clear limits, you create space to thrive without feeling overwhelmed or drained.

11

SETTING HEALTHY BOUNDARIES

"Daring to set boundaries is about having the courage to love ourselves, even when we risk disappointing others." — Brené Brown

When my friend asked me to watch her puppy for the weekend, I hesitated. I knew I needed the weekend to myself, but I also didn't want to upset her. "You're always home!" she said when I gently declined. It stung a little to disappoint her, but I calmly explained that being home didn't mean I was available for pet-sitting. She left frustrated, but by the end of the week, she thanked me. Her brother had stepped in to help, and their weekend together rekindled their bond after years of distance.

That's when it clicked, setting healthy boundaries doesn't make you mean, it makes you smart. As Brené Brown puts it, setting boundaries is an act of self-love, even when it risks disappointing someone else. Saying "no" allowed me to honor my limits and, surprisingly, created space for Anne to reconnect with her family.

Setting boundaries isn't just about drawing lines; it's about knowing your limits and respecting them. Let's explore how you can practice this courage in your own life.

Identifying Your Limits

Recognizing and setting your boundaries is key to protecting your emotional well-being, especially when dealing with rude behavior. By clearly defining your limits, you manage relationships without feeling overwhelmed. Start by reflecting on your core values, as these shape the behaviors you're willing to tolerate. For example, if honesty is vital to you, dishonesty may leave you feeling hurt.

To clarify your boundaries, ask yourself what behaviors make you uncomfortable. Write down situations that trigger these feelings to help spot patterns and better understand where you need to set limits. Identifying your emotional triggers is another crucial step. Notice when you feel angry or upset—these moments reveal your boundaries and allow you to prepare for similar situations calmly.

Once you've identified your boundaries, it's important to communicate them clearly. Use "I" statements like, "I feel frustrated when I'm interrupted," to express yourself without placing blame. Non-verbal cues, such as standing tall or maintaining eye contact, also reinforce your boundaries.

If someone repeatedly crosses the line, restating your boundaries firmly can help. In more serious cases, you may need to distance yourself. Practicing in low-pressure situations builds confidence, making it easier to assert yourself in more challenging scenarios.

Now that you've learned to recognize your boundaries, it's equally important to respect others' limits, fostering healthier and more respectful relationships.

Effective Boundary-Setting Conversations

Bringing up boundaries at the right time is essential for a productive conversation. Choosing the right moment ensures people will hear and understand your message. Avoid discussing boundaries during heated arguments or emotional moments, as it's harder for both people to listen calmly. Instead, opt for a relaxed setting, like a quiet dinner or a peaceful walk. A calm environment fosters open dialogue and makes it easier for the other person to receive your message without getting defensive.

Using "I" statements when talking about boundaries is an effective strategy. It allows you to express your feelings and needs without sounding accusatory, lowering the risk of the other person feeling attacked. For example, rather than saying, "You never respect my time," you could say, "I feel overwhelmed when meetings run over because it affects my schedule." Focusing on your own experience makes it easier for the other person to understand your perspective without feeling blamed, encouraging a more productive and cooperative conversation.

Active listening plays an essential role in these conversations. When you show that the other person's viewpoint matters, they become more willing to hear yours. Active listening means more than just hearing words; it includes engaging through body language and verbal responses. Keep eye contact, nod, and paraphrase their points to show you understand. For example, you could say, "You feel frustrated when I call late at night. Is that correct?" This feedback helps confirm you're aligned and fosters mutual respect.

Staying calm and composed is crucial when talking about boundaries. Feeling anxious when someone crosses your boundaries is natural, but staying calm helps ensure that others hear and understand your message. If emotions rise, take a moment to pause and gather your thoughts. "I need a moment to think" allows you to stay in control and creates a positive atmosphere, signaling you're open to respectful conversation.

Timing plays a crucial role in boundary discussions. Addressing them at the right moment can mean the difference between a productive conversation and an avoidable argument. Pick a time when you're calm and focused, free of distractions. Steer clear of moments when you feel stressed, rushed, or busy. Scheduling the conversation can also be helpful. For example, saying, "Can we talk after dinner when we're both free?" gives you time to prepare, ensuring the conversation stays focused and thoughtful mentally.

Be clear when sharing your concerns and use "I" statements to prevent the other person from feeling attacked. These statements let you express your feelings and needs without placing blame. For example, rather than saying, "You always interrupt me," you could say, "I feel unheard when I'm interrupted during meetings." This method keeps the focus on solving the problem and helps prevent arguments. By expressing your feelings directly, the other person can better understand your perspective and respond with empathy.

Attentive listening plays a crucial role in these discussions. Letting the other person talk is not enough—you must fully engage with what they say. Show you're listening by keeping eye contact, nodding, and offering verbal responses like "I see" or "That makes sense." Reflecting on their words also helps clarify and shows you value their input. For instance, you could say, "So, you're asking for more notice when I make plans that involve you. Is that right?" This kind of engagement creates an open, cooperative atmosphere, making achieving mutual understanding easier.

Staying calm during the conversation is critical to reinforcing the importance of your boundaries. Sensitive topics can trigger emotions, but composure ensures the discussion remains productive. If you start to feel upset, pause, take a breath, and say, "I need a minute to gather my thoughts." This approach shows that the issue matters, and you're committed to finding a solution. Staying calm also reduces tension, making the conversation more effective.

Setting boundaries is crucial, but it's equally important to understand the impact of weak or nonexistent ones. Weak boundaries often cause emotional exhaustion, loss of respect, and strained relationships. Without clear limits, you can face unexpected and harmful consequences that affect your well-being and interactions with others. Strengthening your boundaries is crucial to maintaining your emotional health and ensuring your relationships remain healthy and balanced.

Now that we've covered how to set your boundaries, it's just as important to understand how to respect others' boundaries. Recognizing and honoring the limits set by those around you is vital to maintaining respectful and positive relationships.

Consequences of Weak Boundaries

Failing to set and maintain boundaries can really take a toll on your emotional health and relationships. Without clear boundaries, you might find yourself constantly dealing with interruptions, demands, and even rude behavior, all of which leave you feeling drained. Think about it like this: a teacher who never sets limits with their students would face disruptions all day long, leaving them too exhausted to focus on teaching or even enjoy their personal time. Over time, this emotional exhaustion can lead to burnout, anxiety, or even depression.

Another issue with weak boundaries is that it can lead to a gradual loss of respect from others. If you don't assert yourself, people might assume it's okay to overstep. For example, if you keep accepting extra tasks at work without saying anything, your colleagues may start expecting it regularly. Over time, this erodes your position, leaving you feeling undervalued and leading to resentment. It's the same with personal relationships—saying yes to everything can lead to feelings lack of appreciation and frustration, which ultimately weakens those connections.

Weak boundaries also invite conflict. When limits aren't clear, misunderstandings and disagreements are more likely. Imagine a project manager who doesn't set clear expectations for their team. As deadlines approach, team members may clash over responsibilities, creating unnecessary tension. Setting boundaries helps avoid these issues by clearly defining what you will and won't accept, allowing for smoother interactions both personally and professionally.

Over time, the lack of boundaries wears you down. Without limits on your availability or learning to say no, you'll feel constantly overwhelmed, even when you're supposed to be relaxing. Setting boundaries is about protecting your energy and making room for what truly matters.

Establishing clear boundaries also builds respect. When you politely say no to extra work or stand firm on your time commitments, you're showing others that you value yourself. Over time, this sets the tone for how others treat you, strengthening your relationships and reducing feelings of resentment.

Now that you understand the importance of boundaries for your well-being, the next step is learning to respect others' limits. Just like you, others set boundaries for their emotional health, and responding to them with respect creates healthier, more balanced interactions.

Respecting Others' Boundaries

Respecting the boundaries of others is just as important as setting your own. It's not just about good manners—it's about fostering healthier, more respectful relationships, whether at work, with friends, or with family. By recognizing discomfort, encouraging open conversations, modeling respect, and seeking clarification, you create a positive dynamic that benefits everyone.

People don't always voice their discomfort, so being aware of non-verbal cues is key. If a co-worker becomes quiet or avoids eye contact, they might be feeling uneasy. Crossing arms or fidgeting can also signal discomfort. While it's not necessary to analyze every gesture, paying attention to these signs can help. When you notice them, simply checking in by asking, "Are you okay?" or "Do you need a break?" shows that you respect their boundaries and care about their well-being.

Encouraging open dialogue about boundaries makes it easier to respect others. In both personal and professional settings, fostering a space where people feel safe expressing their needs leads to smoother interactions. For example, asking team members to share their work preferences can prevent misunderstandings, and encouraging friends or family to express when they need space fosters a deeper sense of understanding. This transparency reduces confusion and ensures everyone's boundaries are respected.

Leading by example is another crucial part of respecting boundaries. When you consistently honor other people's limits, you set a positive tone, making it easier for others to follow suit. If a friend says they need time alone, respect that without pushing for more interaction. If a co-worker prefers not to be contacted outside work hours, avoid reaching out during their off-time. By doing so, you show that you take boundaries seriously, and you inspire others to do the same.

In situations where boundaries aren't clear, it's important to ask for clarification. If a colleague reacts unexpectedly to something you said, simply asking, "Did I cross a line?" can clear up any misunderstanding and show that you genuinely care about their comfort. When asking for clarity, be empathetic and non-judgmental—your goal is to understand, not accuse.

Respecting boundaries takes practice, but over time, you'll improve your ability to communicate and interact respectfully. Here are a few practical tips:

- **Pay attention to non-verbal cues**: Body language and tone often reveal discomfort, so be mindful and respond with care.
- **Encourage open communication**: Regularly check in with those around you to create an environment where people feel comfortable sharing their boundaries.
- **Lead by example**: By consistently respecting others' limits, you set a standard that boundaries should always be honored.
- **Ask when in doubt**: If you're unsure about someone's boundaries, ask them directly. It's better to seek clarification than to assume and risk causing discomfort.

Start using these tips in small, everyday interactions. If a colleague seems overwhelmed, take a moment to ask how you can help or respect their need for space. By consistently respecting others' boundaries, you build trust and strengthen relationships, creating a healthier and more positive environment for everyone.

Reflections

What boundaries do you need to set or strengthen to protect your peace and ensure your relationships bring you more balance and fulfillment?

I've realized how essential setting boundaries is for protecting my emotional well-being and enhancing my relationships. Reflecting on my values and journaling about uncomfortable situations gives me clarity on where my limits lie. Recognizing my emotional triggers and tolerance for rudeness helps me manage my reactions more effectively. Using "I" statements and confident body language enables me to communicate my boundaries clearly. Developing an action plan for dealing with repeated violations feels empowering and gives me a sense of control. I also understand that weak boundaries can lead to exhaustion and conflict, so practicing boundary-setting in low-pressure situations helps build my confidence for more challenging conversations.

Now that you've honed your boundary-setting skills, it's time to focus inward. Transformative self-reflection helps you uncover deeper motivations and patterns. By taking time to reflect on your experiences, you'll gain insights that foster personal growth and strengthen your emotional resilience, shaping how you handle future challenges.

12

TRANSFORMATIVE SELF-REFLECTION

"Self-reflection is the school of wisdom." —Baltasar Gracián

After snapping at my friend during what should have been a simple conversation, her stunned silence hit me harder than any words could. It felt like a punch to the gut. Why had I been rude? Later, standing in front of the bathroom mirror, the awkward truth stared back at me: it wasn't about her at all. It was the stress I hadn't dealt with, bubbling up at the wrong moment.

In that instant, I realized something: I was the problem. Not my finest hour, but as Baltasar Gracián reminds us, wisdom comes from self-reflection. Growth often begins with moments of discomfort, doesn't it? It wasn't just about that one mistake; I knew I had to pause and reflect before this behavior turned into a habit I didn't want. Owning your mistakes, however awkward, is where real transformation starts.

That moment got me thinking about the power of journaling. Writing things down before they spiral out of control helps you capture those uncomfortable truths and learn from them. Journaling is like holding a mirror up to your thoughts—it lets you catch patterns, see where you're falling short, and make sure you don't repeat the same mistakes. For me, it became a way to ensure that next time, I could show up for my friend, and myself, with more grace.

Journaling for Self-Awareness

Reflective writing serves as an effective tool for identifying emotional triggers. When you journal, you actively process your thoughts and emotions, not just record them. Putting words on paper helps you step back and see your feelings more easily. It's beneficial when you've dealt with situations that trigger strong emotional responses, like rudeness. By journaling about these encounters, you allow yourself to unpack the frustration and understand why certain situations get under your skin, which leads to healthier ways of reacting.

For example, imagine you've just had a frustrating interaction with a rude co-worker. Carrying that frustration could affect how the rest of your day goes. However, if you take a few moments to write about what happened and how you felt, you create a space to offload that negative energy. You're no longer letting the interaction simmer in your mind; instead, you've confined it to your journal, which can provide relief. Writing externalizes your emotions, making them feel less overwhelming and more like something you can handle.

Reflective writing becomes more insightful when journaling prompts encourage deeper thinking. Questions like "What were my initial reactions to a recent rude encounter?" or "How did I feel in that situation, and why?" help you analyze the experience and better understand your emotional responses. By answering these prompts, you start recognizing patterns in how you react to rudeness or criticism. For example, you might realize you feel more affected when rudeness comes from a superior or occurs in public. These insights provide valuable information to help you manage your reactions better.

A regular journaling practice also lets you track your emotional journey. When you consistently write about your feelings and interactions, you can track your growth and see how much progress you've made in managing your emotions over time. At the beginning of your journaling practice, interacting with a rude customer would leave you angry for hours. Months later, you may respond to a similar situation with greater calm and composure. Going back through old entries can be motivating as you see this progress unfold—proof that you're becoming more emotionally resilient.

Studies have shown that expressive writing can reduce stress and improve mood. According to a study published in 2018, participants who journaled about their emotions experienced significant reductions in anxiety and emotional distress (Smyth et al., 2018). Another survey found that journaling helped participants process trauma, leading to better emotional regulation and resilience (Baikie & Wilhelm, 2005).

Incorporating gratitude into your journaling practice can further enhance its benefits. After writing about a rude encounter, you can shift your focus by listing a few things you're grateful for. Maybe you chatted with a friend or took a peaceful walk that day. Writing down these positive aspects of your life helps balance out the negativity associated with rudeness. Over time, this practice fosters a more optimistic outlook because it encourages you to pay attention to the good things happening around you, even on difficult days.

Remember my friend Sarah, who works as a customer service representative and frequently deals with rude customers. At first, these encounters left her feeling drained, and she would carry that frustration home. But once she started journaling, everything shifted. After each difficult interaction, she took the time to write down what happened and how it made her feel. She used specific prompts, such as "What triggered my anger in this situation?" or "Why did this customer's behavior bother me so much?" Over time, Sarah realized that personal insults provoked a more robust emotional response than general rudeness. This understanding helped her see why certain situations upset her more than others. As she continued journaling, Sarah tracked her emotional progress. A few months later, she handled rude customers more calmly. Her earlier journal entries were frustrating, but the later ones showed a more balanced response. Additionally, by adding gratitude to her writing, Sarah shifted her outlook. She started noticing kind customers and supportive colleagues, which helped her balance the adverse interactions that used to dominate her thoughts.

Why Do Rude People Piss Me Off!

You can quickly start a journaling practice by setting aside a few minutes each day to reflect on your experiences and emotions. Begin with simple observations about how your day went and how specific interactions made you feel. As you get more comfortable, you can use journaling prompts to dig deeper into specific emotional triggers, such as rudeness. Ask yourself, "How did I react to that rude remark today?" or "Why did I feel so angry?" You can also add a section for gratitude at the end of each entry to help shift your focus toward the positive. The key is consistency. The more often you journal, the more insights you'll gain into your emotional patterns and the more resilient you'll become.

Reflective writing helps you gain control over your emotional responses and leads to personal growth. But it's not the only practice that can improve how you handle challenging situations like rudeness. Meditation is a valuable tool for building emotional awareness and lowering stress. Incorporating meditation into your daily routine can enhance your emotional resilience and help you learn to respond to challenging interactions with greater calm and clarity.

The Role of Meditation

Meditation can be a game-changer when managing emotions and staying focused during rude interactions. It gives you tools to handle those challenging moments with composure. One of the main benefits of meditation is that it helps you recognize your emotions without letting them take over. By practicing regularly, you become more aware of how your mind and body react to stress, giving you that crucial moment to pause before responding. So, instead of instantly snapping back at a rude comment, you learn to breathe, process, and choose a more thoughtful response.

In heated situations, this pause can make all the difference. Let's say someone says something rude to you, your first instinct might be to fire back. But with meditation, you can catch those early signs of anger, like a racing heart or tight chest, and pause before saying something you'll regret. That brief pause can completely shift how the interaction plays out, leading to a calmer, more measured outcome.

Visualization also works wonders alongside meditation. Picture that co-worker who always makes snide comments. By visualizing yourself staying calm and collected in those moments, you create a mental game plan. Then, when the situation happens, you'll be more likely to stick to your cool response rather than get swept away by emotions.

Even short meditation sessions can improve emotional control. Research shows that brief mindfulness meditation (BMM) can help reduce emotional reactivity, making it easier to stay calm during stressful moments, like when dealing with rude behavior.

Meditation sharpens your focus, too. In tense situations, it's easy to get swept up in emotions and lose track of your goal. With meditation, you stay grounded in what you want to achieve, whether resolving a conflict peacefully or just staying calm until the conversation is over. Having that clarity helps you respond with intention, even when faced with rudeness.

It also helps you recognize the deeper emotions that rudeness can stir up. Sometimes, rude behavior brings up insecurities, fears, or memories of past experiences. Meditation helps you see those underlying emotions and manage them. For example, if a customer makes a snarky comment, it might remind you of times when you felt undervalued. Recognizing this allows you to manage your reaction more effectively, making it less likely that future rude interactions will trigger the same emotional response.

If you work in customer service, it's natural to feel defensive when dealing with rude clients. But meditation helps you realize that your frustration might be about more than just the client's behavior, it could be tied to deeper issues, like feeling unappreciated at work. Once you're aware of this, you can address the root cause instead of letting rude encounters overwhelm you.

Studies support the benefits of meditation for emotional regulation and resilience. Research shows that regular meditation can lower stress and improve emotional stability (Ede et al., 2020), making it easier to keep your cool in tough situations.

And here's the good news: meditation doesn't have to take much time. Start with just five minutes a day, and you'll notice a difference. Apps like Calm and Headspace offer guided meditations that are easy to follow, even for beginners. If you prefer more structure, mindfulness-based stress reduction (MBSR) programs or group meditation classes can offer additional support, helping you build emotional resilience in a more guided, community-based setting.

As you work on building emotional resilience through meditation, another step is seeking feedback from trusted sources. Sometimes it's hard to see if your reactions are balanced, especially when dealing with repeated rudeness. Gaining an outside perspective from colleagues, friends, or mentors can help you evaluate how you're handling these situations and identify areas for improvement. Constructive feedback after a tough interaction can show you what you did well and where you can grow.

Seeking Feedback From Trusted Sources

When it comes to handling rude interactions, it's important to understand your personal biases and how they affect your responses. It's completely normal to feel frustrated when someone is rude, but recognizing your triggers is a key step toward building emotional resilience. Sometimes, though, it's tough to see those patterns on your own. That's where getting feedback from trusted people in your life, friends, family, or even colleagues, can be a real game-changer.

Imagine asking a close friend for their honest take on how you handle rude situations. They might point out things you hadn't noticed, like how certain comments always get under your skin. Once you're aware of these triggers, you'll have a much better shot at managing your reactions before they turn into frustration or anger. It's about gaining awareness that can help you stay calm when rude situations arise.

Talking openly with others about your experiences also creates space for growth. Sharing those stories, like that rude comment your colleague made last week, with someone else can bring fresh insights. Maybe they've dealt with something similar and can offer a new perspective on how to handle it next time. Having these conversations not only gives you practical advice but also reminds you that you're not in this alone.

Getting external feedback from others doesn't replace your own self-reflection; instead, it complements it. By building a support system, whether it's friends, mentors, or family, you can get diverse perspectives that help you handle difficult situations more smoothly. When you know that others are rooting for your growth, it feels less isolating, and you can face challenging moments with more confidence and resilience.

Now, if you're really looking to step up your game in managing rude interactions, seeking advice from people who are skilled in emotional intelligence can be super helpful. For example, a mentor could suggest some role-playing exercises to practice how you'd respond calmly under pressure or help you develop strategies to avoid reacting impulsively. This is especially useful in tricky environments like the workplace, where stress levels are often high. By strengthening your emotional intelligence, you'll not only reduce your stress but likely boost your overall job satisfaction, too.

Another great way to expand your emotional toolkit is by understanding where other people are coming from. Often, we assume the worst about someone's rude behavior, but the truth is, we usually don't know the full story. Maybe that rude colleague is going through a rough time, or the person who snapped at you is stressed out. Taking a moment to consider what might be happening in their life can help you respond with more empathy and less frustration. Shifting your perspective in this way can lead to a more balanced response and help you maintain your peace.

It's also helpful to expose yourself to different viewpoints. By engaging with people from various backgrounds or reading diverse perspectives, you become more open-minded and understanding in general. Whether it's through a podcast, a book, or just a chat with someone who sees the world differently, these experiences can really broaden your emotional range. You'll be better equipped to handle rudeness with grace because you'll understand that everyone's carrying something you might not see.

Finally, if you're dealing with a particularly difficult situation, sometimes it's worth seeking advice from someone outside your usual circle. Maybe a friend from a different background or a mentor can offer insights you hadn't thought of. They might help you see things from a completely new angle. This collaborative approach not only helps you find a solution but also strengthens your emotional resilience by reminding you that you've got people who support you.

Remember, handling rude behavior isn't something you have to figure out overnight. It's a journey, and each time you practice staying calm and grounded, you're getting a little better at it. Keep an open mind, seek feedback from others, and continue growing. With time, you'll find that managing rude situations becomes easier, and you'll feel more confident in your ability to protect your peace.

Continuous Personal Growth

Viewing personal development as a journey can change how you respond to rude behavior. When you see growth as an ongoing process, every rude encounter becomes a chance to learn and improve. Instead of letting negativity weigh you down, you can use it as fuel for personal progress.

Adopting a growth mindset is key here. Research by Dr. Carol Dweck shows that people who view challenges as learning opportunities, rather than failures, build resilience. Applying this to rude situations means reflecting on your reactions, learning from them, and becoming stronger for the next time.

Setting specific goals can also help. For example, you could aim to stay calm during five consecutive rude encounters. Achieving that goal proves progress and boosts your motivation. You can also track how each small success adds to your personal development.

Being flexible with your approach is another valuable tool. Techniques like active listening, humor, or empathy can be game-changers. Studies show that people who use active listening in conflicts often get better outcomes because they focus on understanding the other person. In a rude interaction, listening carefully might reveal what's really behind someone's behavior, allowing you to respond more thoughtfully.

It's also important to celebrate small victories. Maybe you stayed calm when a customer got upset, or diffused a tense situation at work. Recognizing these moments builds confidence and motivates you to keep growing.

For example, if a colleague is consistently rude, you might start by setting a goal to take a deep breath before responding. Over time, you could experiment with different strategies like calmly stating how their words make you feel. As you start to see improvements—like fewer arguments or a better relationship—those small victories will encourage you to keep moving forward.

Building emotional resilience this way not only helps at work but in all areas of life. Research shows that people who develop resilience experience better mental health, job satisfaction, and lower stress. By practicing patience, trying new approaches, and celebrating wins, you strengthen your ability to handle rudeness in any setting.

Finally, remember that growth takes time. It's okay to have setbacks, and self-compassion is essential on this journey. Just as you're learning, so is everyone else. By giving yourself grace, you're more likely to bounce back quickly and continue improving, even when things get tough.

Whether you're handling a rude customer or dealing with difficult people at work, adopting a growth mindset, setting goals, and celebrating small wins can help you navigate challenging situations with confidence and calm.

Reflections

How can you adapt your emotional toolkit, including journaling, meditation, and visualization, to better manage challenging interactions in both your personal and professional life?

I've come to understand the critical importance of managing my emotional responses, especially in challenging situations. Journaling has been an anchor in this process, allowing me to track my progress and recognize how much I've grown over time. Meditation, too, has become a key tool, helping me create that necessary pause before reacting and find a sense of calm amidst the chaos. Visualization exercises, combined with honest feedback from trusted friends, have equipped me with fresh perspectives, making difficult interactions feel less personal and more manageable.

Looking forward, I'm excited to explore how these techniques can be applied in different areas of my life, from the workplace to personal relationships, adapting my approach based on the context. Each scenario offers a new opportunity to strengthen my emotional toolkit. Let's now dive into applying these strategies across various settings and deepening our understanding of resilient, compassionate responses.

13

HANDLING RUDE BEHAVIOR ACROSS DIFFERENT CONTEXTS

"When they go low, we go high." – Michelle Obama

I was in a meeting when a colleague, made a snarky comment about my project: "Well, that's one way to do it, I guess." It was unnecessary and left a sour taste in the room. My initial reaction was to snap back, but I paused. Instead of letting his words derail the discussion, I responded calmly, "Thanks for the feedback, let's talk after the meeting about how we can improve it together."

He looked surprised, and the tension eased. I realized that, by staying composed and professional, I set the tone for the rest of the team. It wasn't about winning the argument; it was about keeping the focus on collaboration and problem-solving.

This moment reminded me that rudeness and negativity, whether in the workplace or at home, have a ripple effect. But so do grace and composure. By choosing to "go high," you don't just protect your peace, you create a positive example for others to follow.

Let's dive into how we can harness this mindset to navigate rudeness gracefully, keeping our cool and setting the standard for better interactions.

Workplace Dynamics

Handling rudeness at work isn't just about staying professional, it's about creating a respectful and productive environment for everyone. Every workplace has its own unique culture that shapes how employees interact, and understanding that culture is key to addressing rude behavior. In fast-paced or high-pressure environments, rudeness can sometimes become a coping mechanism or even a way for people to assert control. But recognizing these patterns early on can help prevent rudeness from becoming the norm.

The Impact of Rude Behavior

Did you know that dealing with rudeness at work doesn't just affect the person on the receiving end? A study from Georgetown University found that employees who experience rudeness are less engaged—66% reduce their effort, and 25% take their frustration out on customers (Porath & Pearson, 2013). So, it's not just about an offhand comment; rudeness can ripple through the whole organization, dragging down morale and productivity.

The Power of Clear Communication

One of the best ways to prevent rudeness from escalating is clear communication. Using "I" statements when discussing conflicts helps lower defensiveness and keeps conversations focused on solutions. For example, instead of saying, "You never meet deadlines," try, "Missed deadlines frustrate me because they impact my schedule." It's a subtle shift that keeps the conversation respectful.

Active listening is another big part of this. If a colleague makes a rude comment, try paraphrasing what they've said. If someone remarks, "We should've finished this by now," you can respond with, "It sounds like you're feeling stressed about the timeline." Acknowledging their feelings helps defuse tension and keeps the conversation civil.

Emotional Control in Difficult Situations

When rudeness happens, emotional self-control is key. It's easy to react impulsively, but that can make things worse. Take a moment to breathe, gather your thoughts, and respond calmly. And if things get too heated, it's okay to excuse yourself to cool down. Once you've regained your composure, you'll be in a much better position to handle the situation effectively.

Promoting Kindness in the Workplace

Small acts of kindness can make a big difference in preventing rudeness from taking root. Recognizing a colleague's hard work or simply showing appreciation can have a ripple effect. In fact, a 2017 Gallup study found that workplaces where employees feel appreciated experience a 21% boost in productivity (How to Increase Productivity by 21% With Employee Engagement, 2019). Encouraging kindness not only improves morale but also creates a more respectful and supportive work environment.

Offering support when a colleague feels disrespected can also go a long way. Sometimes, just listening to someone who's had a rough day helps them feel seen and supported, which strengthens team dynamics and promotes respect.

Leadership's Role in Shaping Workplace Culture

Leadership plays a huge role in setting the tone for workplace behavior. When managers model respectful behavior and quickly address rudeness, it sends a clear message that incivility won't be tolerated. Christine Porath, an expert on workplace behavior, says that "rude behavior, when left unchecked, can spread like a virus, affecting the overall workplace climate" (Porath, 2017). Leaders must walk the talk and ensure that respect is at the core of all interactions.

Effective Communication Strategies

Clear communication is essential when managing conflicts. Asking open-ended questions can turn a tense conversation into a productive one. Instead of saying, "Why did you miss the deadline?" try, "Can you tell me what challenges you faced with the deadline?" This way, you're inviting conversation and reducing defensiveness.

Non-verbal communication also matters. Simple actions like making eye contact, nodding, or maintaining an open posture show that you're listening and engaged. These small gestures help create a more respectful environment.

Addressing Emotional Reactions

Managing emotional reactions to rudeness is a skill that can be honed through emotional intelligence training. Many companies that invest in these programs see improvements in employee satisfaction and retention. Christine Porath's TED Talk also highlights how maintaining composure during incivility leads to better career outcomes and stronger professional relationships (Crowley, 2018). Giving employees the tools to handle rudeness effectively creates a more positive and resilient workplace..

Building a Respectful Culture

Creating a respectful workplace requires effort from both individuals and the collective team. Open conversations about the importance of respect help raise awareness and reinforce positive behavior. Some companies have even introduced "kindness committees" to monitor workplace behavior and tackle incivility head-on. This proactive approach sends a strong message that respect matters.

Incorporating respect into your organization's core values can further emphasize its importance. Employees should feel empowered to speak up about rude behavior without fear of retaliation, knowing they're part of a culture that values their well-being.

Speaking of social interactions, how do we handle rudeness in personal settings? Whether at a family gathering or a social event, tricky behavior can surface. Let's explore how to navigate these situations with humor and grace.

Navigating Social Gatherings

Addressing rudeness in social settings is all about keeping things positive and strengthening your relationships. Rude behavior, whether it's a snide remark or someone cutting you off in conversation, can catch you off guard. But knowing how to recognize and handle it gracefully can make all the difference. In this section, we'll explore ways to spot rudeness, respond calmly, use humor to ease the tension, set boundaries, and even turn those rude moments into chances for deeper connections.

Recognizing Rudeness and Responding Gracefully

The first step in handling rudeness is recognizing it. In social settings, this might look like someone interrupting you, making a snarky joke, or dismissing what you say. It's helpful to tell the difference between intentional rudeness and harmless slips, sometimes people genuinely don't realize how their words come across. For instance, a friend might make an offhand comment without any intention of hurting your feelings.

Before responding, take a beat to think it over and consider your relationship with the person. If you react impulsively, it can worsen the situation. But if it's someone close to you, a gentle approach often works. For example, saying something like, "I know you didn't mean it, but that comment kind of stung," opens the door to a constructive conversation rather than more conflict.

Studies also suggest that staying calm when confronted with rudeness can reduce stress (The Outsized Impacts of Rudeness in the Workplace, 2021). The same idea applies to social settings, a quick pause to assess the situation can help prevent escalation and keep the interaction civil.

Using Humor to Lighten the Mood

Humor can be a fantastic tool for defusing tension in social situations. It shifts the focus away from negativity, manages conflict, and lowers stress. Thoughtful humor, especially, can gently address rudeness without direct confrontation.

For instance, if someone makes a snide comment about your outfit, instead of getting defensive, you could playfully reply, "Well, I guess I'll stand out tonight!" This keeps things light and shows the comment didn't bother you. Often, humor is a subtle way to make people realize they've crossed a line.

The key is to keep the humor gentle and avoid sarcasm, which can backfire. Aim for humor that softens the interaction and redirects the conversation in a positive direction. When used right, humor can turn a rude encounter into a friendly exchange

Clear Boundaries

Not everyone realizes when they're being rude. Some people think they're just being "blunt" or "playful" and may not see the impact of their words. That's where clear communication can help. Calmly expressing what bothers you helps others understand how you'd like to be treated.

Using "I" statements works well here. Instead of saying, "You're always interrupting me," try, "I feel disrespected when I'm interrupted." This way, you're talking about how you feel rather than accusing the other person, which helps prevent defensiveness.

It's often best to address these issues in private. Pulling the person aside to explain how their actions affect you is generally more effective than calling them out in front of others. Most people appreciate a respectful approach and are more open to adjusting their behavior once they understand its impact.

Research shows that setting boundaries in social interactions can boost confidence and self-respect (Roggero, 2023). By calmly explaining your feelings, you're not only protecting yourself but also fostering mutual respect.

Transforming Rude Encounters Into Opportunities for Deeper Connections

Believe it or not, rude encounters can sometimes lead to healthier relationships. They offer a chance to address underlying issues and consider each other's viewpoints. When approached with patience and empathy, these moments can build trust and mutual respect.

For example, if a friend makes a hurtful joke, it can open up a conversation about the kinds of humor that work within your group. Addressing the comment directly helps clear up misunderstandings and sets a standard for future interactions. Not only does this prevent similar issues, but it also shows that you value maintaining respect.

Studies suggest that openly addressing uncomfortable situations can actually lead to deeper, more meaningful connections (Blachnio, 2021). When people feel comfortable discussing awkward or rude moments, it builds a sense of safety and honesty within the group. By sharing your feelings, you can encourage others to do the same, creating a more supportive and open environment.

Approaching these situations with empathy can turn a negative moment into a meaningful conversation about boundaries and respect. Taking time to reflect on why someone behaved rudely, maybe they were stressed or didn't understand the social context, can help you respond with understanding. This approach can strengthen your relationships and promote better communication.

Now, let's shift focus to another area where behavior can make a big difference, family interactions. Just like in social settings, dealing with difficult family dynamics requires patience, compassion, and clear communication. How we approach challenging moments with family can make all the difference in creating a harmonious home environment.

Family Interactions

Handling rudeness with family can be tough. Because we're so deeply connected to our family members, the history and expectations we share can add layers of complexity to every interaction. Family relationships can offer comfort and security, but they can also lead to hurt feelings, especially when conversations take a negative turn. Learning to respond with respect and compassion in those tense moments is key to keeping family bonds strong.

Recognizing Family Roles and Patterns

Family roles and history often shape our interactions. Maybe you're the "responsible older sibling" or the "peacekeeper," roles that can sometimes lead to tension. These patterns, while familiar, can make certain conflicts feel almost inevitable. For example, an older sibling might take on a protective (or even bossy) role, causing friction. Or, parents might pass down unintentional communication habits that can come across as rude or dismissive. Recognizing these dynamics can help you approach family interactions with a bit more patience.

Reflecting on family history can also help you understand recurring conflicts. If your family tends to be competitive, for instance, you might find passive-aggressive comments or jabs happening regularly. Recognizing these patterns helps you find ways to handle rudeness without taking it too personally.

Research shows that families with clear hierarchical structures often face ongoing conflicts because of power imbalances (Cohen, 2023). By understanding these dynamics, you can approach conversations more thoughtfully and keep the peace.

Responding With Compassion

It's natural to feel hurt or frustrated when a family member says something rude. But reacting with sarcasm or anger usually only escalates things. Responding with compassion instead can go a long way. This doesn't mean excusing bad behavior; it just means recognizing that their words might stem from stress or personal issues.

For instance, if a family member makes a hurtful comment about your career, instead of snapping back, you could say, "I hear your concerns. Can we talk about this calmly?" This response opens up a more productive conversation while acknowledging their emotions. Compassionate responses can improve relationships by creating space for understanding.

Taking a moment to pause before responding can help. Take a deep breath, collect your thoughts, and try to see things from their perspective. Research shows that empathy leads to better conflict resolution by making everyone feel heard (Baer, 2017).

Adjusting Your Expectations

Dealing with family also means adjusting your expectations. It's unrealistic to expect perfect behavior, especially at big gatherings when emotions are high. Accepting that some rudeness may happen can help you manage your own responses. This doesn't mean tolerating mistreatment, it's about being realistic about what you can control.

Before a family event, mentally prepare by setting manageable expectations. If you know that certain topics, like politics or finances, tend to lead to arguments, plan to steer clear of them. You could also prepare neutral responses for common rude remarks. For example, if someone always comments on your career, a simple "I'd rather not discuss that today" can keep things calm.

Adjusting your expectations also helps you keep perspective. Families aren't perfect, and conflicts are a natural part of the experience. Family therapy suggests that reframing your expectations can help you stay emotionally resilient in challenging situations.

Offering Constructive Feedback

If rude behavior becomes a pattern, offering constructive feedback can help improve communication. But how you say it matters. Direct criticism often puts people on the defensive, so try using "I" statements instead. For example, saying, "I feel hurt when you interrupt me," focuses on your feelings without sounding like an accusation.

Timing is also key. Bringing up an issue in the heat of the moment usually isn't productive. Wait until you're both calm, and pair your feedback with something positive. You might say, "I appreciated how supportive you were earlier. Can we keep that tone in future conversations?" This approach encourages change while keeping the tone positive.

Offering practical solutions can also be helpful. If a family member frequently interrupts, for example, you could suggest, "Let's try taking turns so everyone gets a chance to speak." Clear suggestions show that you're committed to improving communication.

Studies show that giving feedback in a non-confrontational way increases the chances of positive change. Regular family check-ins can also help create a safe space for addressing issues, reducing the chances of rude behavior during informal gatherings.

Practical Guidelines

- **Recognize family dynamics:** Reflect on your family's roles and history. Are there patterns or conflicts that repeatedly lead to rude interactions? Recognizing these patterns is the first step toward managing them.
- **Compassionate responses:** Pause before reacting, and try to approach the situation with empathy. For instance, if a family member criticizes you, respond with, "I see you're upset. Can we talk about this calmly?"
- **Adjust expectations:** Accept that some level of rudeness may happen and prepare for it. For example, steer clear of topics like politics if they tend to lead to conflict.
- **Positive reinforcement:** Pair constructive feedback with positive comments. For example, "I appreciated your support earlier. Can we keep that tone in future conversations?"

Learning to recognize and address these patterns can make a big difference in handling rudeness within your family. By staying compassionate, adjusting your expectations, and offering constructive feedback, you can foster healthier family dynamics and reduce the emotional toll of rude interactions.

Now that we've covered family dynamics, let's talk about dealing with rudeness in public spaces, where a lack of personal history can add a whole new layer of complexity.

Public Spaces Challenges

Dealing with rudeness in public spaces is, unfortunately, part of today's fast-paced world. We've all seen it—someone cutting in line, raising their voice at a cashier, or showing road rage. These encounters can be frustrating and catch you off guard. Learning how to handle these moments gracefully helps you stay calm and maintain your dignity.

Recognizing Rude Behaviors

The first step in handling rudeness is recognizing it for what it is. People often act out in busy places because they're stressed or rushed. Common signs of rudeness include things like aggressive gestures, disrespectful comments, or inconsiderate actions, such as cutting in line or talking loudly in a quiet space.

For example, you might be waiting at the bank, and someone skips the line entirely to go straight to the teller. Or you're at a library, and someone's having a loud conversation, ignoring the usual rules of silence. Noticing these behaviors early can help you mentally prepare, making it easier to stay calm and avoid a knee-jerk reaction.

Maintaining Composure

When you encounter rude behavior, keeping your cool is essential. It's easy to feel defensive or angry, but reacting emotionally often makes things worse. A good trick is to take a pause, breathe deeply and count to ten before deciding how to respond. This short pause helps you stay grounded and choose a calm response.

Practicing empathy can also help you stay calm. People often act rudely when they're stressed or dealing with personal struggles. For example, if someone snaps at a server, it might not be about the service at all, they could be going through a rough patch in their personal life. Reminding yourself that their behavior might reflect their own issues, not you, can make it easier to let things go.

Responding with kindness or neutrality can also help. Imagine someone bumps into you and doesn't apologize. Instead of reacting angrily, you could just step aside and let it go, which might even prompt them to realize their mistake and apologize. Often, people mirror the emotions they see, so your calmness might lead them to adjust their own behavior.

Choosing When to Respond

Sometimes, the best response to rude behavior is no response at all. Not every situation requires you to engage. Ignoring the behavior might be the best choice, especially if the person seems confrontational or unstable. Your peace and safety come first.

For instance, if someone on public transportation is loudly ranting, it's usually better to move seats rather than confront them. This way, you avoid unnecessary conflict and save your energy for more meaningful interactions.

However, there are times when addressing the behavior is necessary, especially if it directly affects you. In these cases, staying calm but assertive is crucial. Using "I" statements can help you communicate your feelings without sounding accusatory. For example, if someone speaks to you disrespectfully, saying, "I feel uncomfortable when you talk to me like that," keeps the focus on your feelings and lowers the chance of escalation.

Prioritizing Self-Care

After dealing with rude behavior, taking time for self-care is essential. Negative interactions can be draining, but practicing positive affirmations can help you regain balance. Studies show that negative experiences have a stronger impact than positive ones, by a ratio of about 5-to-1 (Benson, 2017). So, after a negative encounter, it's helpful to remind yourself of five positive things to counterbalance the experience.

Doing something you enjoy, whether it's going for a walk, listening to music, or catching up with friends, can also help reset your mood and bring back some positivity.

Setting Boundaries

Setting boundaries is a powerful way to handle rudeness. Sometimes, simply letting someone know what you won't tolerate can stop disrespectful behavior. For example, if someone keeps making rude comments in a social setting, you could calmly say, "I don't like being spoken to that way." This shows that you respect yourself and sets a clear line against disrespect.

Setting boundaries isn't about being confrontational, it's about protecting your emotional well-being. Clear boundaries can help reduce misunderstandings and improve communication.

Active Listening and Assertiveness

Combining active listening with assertiveness can also help in public situations. Acknowledging someone's frustration can sometimes calm them down. For example, if someone's complaining rudely about slow service, you might say, "I understand it's frustrating. Let's work on finding a solution." This shows empathy but keeps the conversation constructive.

If a customer complains rudely at a restaurant, calmly acknowledging their frustration while saying, "We're all waiting for our food," shows you understand but won't entertain unnecessary negativity. This balance of empathy and assertiveness can set respectful boundaries without adding tension.

Building Emotional Resilience

Regular exposure to rudeness can be exhausting, so it's essential to build emotional resilience. Resilience helps you bounce back from negative interactions more quickly. A solid support system, friends or family you can vent to after a tough day, can lighten the emotional load.

Physical activities like running, yoga, or even a brisk walk can also boost resilience. Studies show that regular exercise enhances emotional resilience, helping people manage stress more effectively (Neumann et al., 2022).

Learning From Each Encounter

Finally, viewing each rude encounter as a learning opportunity can empower you. Reflecting on how you responded and thinking about different ways to handle similar situations can help you find more effective strategies over time. Soon, managing rude encounters will feel more natural, and you'll be able to respond with confidence and calmness.

Each experience helps refine your approach, and as your emotional toolkit grows, you'll find these encounters become less stressful, allowing you to move through your day with ease.

Reflections

How can you use empathy, assertiveness, and self-care to transform difficult encounters into opportunities for personal growth and stronger connections with others?

I've learned that rudeness can appear in many areas of life, at work, with family, and in public spaces and is often rooted in stress or competition. I've come to realize just how important clear communication and emotional control are when dealing with difficult people. By using tools like "I" statements, asking open-ended questions, and setting clear boundaries, I can prevent misunderstandings and foster more respectful interactions. These techniques create space for understanding and help me respond thoughtfully instead of reacting impulsively.

Encouraging kindness and practicing emotional intelligence have made a noticeable difference in my relationships, improving not just my own well-being but also my connections with others. I'm also learning that handling rude encounters with empathy, assertiveness, and self-care doesn't just help me in the moment—it's helping me grow emotionally and develop resilience for the future. Taking time to recharge, whether through a walk, a talk with a friend, or simply pausing to breathe, helps me maintain that resilience when dealing with difficult people.

As I continue to apply these insights, I'm excited to share these strategies with others. By offering empathy and support to those facing similar challenges, I hope to create an environment where everyone feels valued, even when interactions are difficult. Each step on this path reinforces that we can all contribute to a more respectful and understanding world.

14

HELPING OTHERS MANAGE RUDENESS

"People will forget what you said, people will forget what you did, but people will never forget how you made them feel." – Maya Angelou

The other day, my friend and I were watching a movie at her place when her cousin kept interrupting with comments about the plot. After the third interruption, I calmly said, "If the characters could hear you, they'd tell you to pipe down and let them act." She laughed, rolled her eyes, and, thankfully, quieted down. We finished the movie in peace. It wasn't a big moment, but it reminded me how powerful even a small, lighthearted response can be. Her cousin didn't feel scolded, and we all enjoyed the rest of the evening.

It got me thinking while humor worked here, sometimes what someone really needs isn't a witty comeback, but genuine support, a friend who listens and validates their feelings. Both approaches can make a lasting impact, depending on the situation.

Maya Angelou's words resonate deeply here. Whether through laughter or empathy, how we handle rude behavior shapes how others feel long after the moment has passed. In this chapter, let's explore how to support the people around us as they navigate rude encounters, learning when to ease tension with humor and when to offer a compassionate ear. One thoughtful response at a time, we can help create more positive, lasting experiences.

Offering Emotional Support

Dealing with rude behavior can be tough, but offering a bit of emotional support can make a world of difference for someone navigating these situations. Emotional support doesn't just help them process their feelings; it builds resilience and strengthens relationships over time.

Validating Emotions

The first step in supporting someone emotionally is validating their feelings. When someone encounters rude behavior, feeling frustrated, hurt, or even angry is completely natural. Acknowledging those emotions shows them they're understood and accepted. For example, if a co-worker shares that they're upset about a rude comment during a meeting, simply saying, "Wow, that sounds frustrating," can mean a lot. Studies show that when people feel heard and validated, they tend to calm down faster (Yu et al., 2021). Ignoring or brushing off these emotions often leads to bigger issues later, so validating is a powerful first step.

Encouraging Expression

Another key part of emotional support is letting the person express how they feel. Sometimes, people just need to vent without getting a solution right away. For instance, if a friend had a rough day at work dealing with a rude customer, give them space to let it all out instead of jumping in with advice. Listening can be a big relief for them. Research shows that talking about tough experiences can significantly reduce stress (Dreher, 2019). It's not always about fixing things; it's about showing up and offering empathy.

Active Listening

Active listening is huge when it comes to offering support. This means you're truly focused on what they're saying, not just the words but the feelings behind them. When someone's venting about rude behavior, they usually just want to feel heard. For example, if a family member comes home frustrated after dealing with a rude boss, giving them your full attention—nodding, keeping eye contact, or even summarizing what they've shared—can reassure them that you're there for them. Listening with empathy also supports mental health since feeling heard can reduce anxiety and build a sense of connection.

Focusing on Positivity

While it's essential to validate and listen, gently helping someone shift their focus toward the positives can also lighten their load. This doesn't mean ignoring their feelings; it's about helping them see the good things in their life alongside the bad. If a co-worker is feeling down after a harsh client interaction, you could remind them of a recent success or compliment their work. Focusing on positive moments helps balance out the emotional strain of rudeness. Research shows that people who focus on the positives tend to be more resilient and less affected by everyday stressors (Cherry, 2023).

Building Resilience

Helping someone build resilience means encouraging them to see rude encounters as growth opportunities. Psychologist Sharon Grossman suggests that viewing stressors like rude customers or co-workers as challenges (rather than threats) helps build resilience over time (Grossman, n.d.). Think about mental health professionals, they often deal with difficult clients, but these interactions help them develop stronger communication and coping skills. You can encourage others to see rude behavior as a chance to strengthen their own emotional resilience, too.

Developing Coping Mechanisms

Resilience also involves having a few solid coping mechanisms. One helpful strategy is to reframe rude encounters as learning moments. For example, dealing with a demanding customer might help someone practice conflict resolution. Sharing your own experiences with handling rudeness can inspire others to view these situations constructively. If you've ever turned a rude interaction into a learning experience, sharing how you did it can encourage others to do the same. Reframing these encounters can boost emotional resilience and reduce stress.

Strengthening Relationships

Having strong relationships can make it easier to handle the emotional toll of rudeness. At work, having a supportive team can make all the difference. If you're part of a group where people genuinely support each other, rude comments or behavior from clients or supervisors don't sting as much. Studies show that employees with strong social support experience less stress and burnout, even when they're dealing with difficult situations. Creating this kind of supportive environment can act as a buffer against the emotional impact of rudeness.

Personal relationships also play a big role in offering emotional support. When you know you have a trusted friend or family member to turn to, it makes handling rude encounters easier. Regular check-ins with loved ones and keeping those connections strong ensure you'll always have someone to lean on when tough times arise. Research backs this up, finding that people with strong personal connections are better able to handle stress, including the impact of rudeness (Manage Stress: Strengthen Your Support Network, 2019).

Cultivating Empathy for the Rude Person

As hard as it can be, cultivating empathy for the person being rude can sometimes make things easier. Rudeness often stems from the other person's stress, frustration, or personal struggles. While it doesn't excuse their behavior, it can help you see the situation from a different perspective. Mental health experts note that rudeness can sometimes be a symptom of issues like anxiety or trauma. Realizing that the person may be projecting their pain can help you respond with patience and avoid taking things personally. Employees who show empathy toward rude co-workers also tend to experience less burnout.

Let's move on to some practical strategies for handling rude behavior in the long term. These tips can help you and others feel more equipped to deal with challenging interactions.

Sharing Effective Strategies

Helping others manage rudeness is an incredibly useful skill, whether you're in the workplace, an educator, or just someone who regularly deals with difficult people. From a snappy co-worker to a demanding client or a student testing limits, knowing how to respond can help keep the peace and create a more positive environment. Here are some practical techniques you can share to help others build their coping skills and offer meaningful support when rudeness arises

Communication Techniques

One of the most effective tools for handling rudeness is good communication. When someone's rude, our first instinct might be to get defensive or even respond with similar behavior, but that often just escalates things. Instead, encourage a calm, assertive approach. One helpful strategy is using "I" statements, which allow you to express your feelings without placing blame.

For example, instead of saying, "You're being rude," try, "I feel upset when you talk to me that way." This approach puts the focus on how the behavior impacts you and keeps the conversation open. Research backs this up, showing that "I" statements are more likely to lead to a constructive resolution (Sehat, 2023).

Active listening is another key tool. Rude behavior often comes from frustration or feeling unheard. When you take the time to listen, you might uncover what's really going on and find common ground. For instance, if a colleague snaps at you during a stressful meeting, you could respond, "It sounds like something's bothering you. Want to talk about it?" This opens the door to a conversation instead of an argument.

Nonverbal communication is just as important. Neutral body language, like nodding and keeping eye contact, shows respect for the other person's perspective, even if you don't agree with their behavior. Studies show that calm body language, steady eye contact, and a neutral tone of voice can help de-escalate tense situations (Hanson, 2021).

Setting Boundaries

Setting clear, consistent boundaries is essential when managing rudeness. Boundaries let others know what's okay and what isn't without being confrontational. They protect your emotional well-being and teach others how you expect to be treated. For example, you might say, "I'm happy to keep talking, but I won't engage if voices are raised." This statement sets a clear limit while still keeping the conversation open.

Consistency is key. If you don't stick to your boundaries, others may assume the behavior is acceptable and keep repeating it. Role-playing can be a helpful way to show others how to set boundaries. For example, if a co-worker frequently interrupts, you could practice a response like, "I'd appreciate it if we could each take turns speaking." Practicing this helps you stay calm and assertive without getting emotional.

Boundaries also apply to your time, especially with remote work becoming so common. If someone contacts you outside work hours with a non-urgent issue, it's okay to say, "I need this time for myself; let's catch up during office hours." This kind of boundary protects your mental well-being and shows you value your time. Research shows that setting boundaries, particularly at work, boosts emotional health and helps prevent burnout (Martin, 2022).

Using Humor

Humor can be a powerful way to manage rudeness and ease tension, but it needs to be used thoughtfully. A well-timed joke can defuse a situation, but a poorly timed one might make things worse. If used wisely, humor can make rude comments feel less intense.

For example, if a customer complains about a wait time, a light-hearted comment like, "Looks like our coffee machine isn't quite rocket-speed today!" can lighten the mood. This kind of humor acknowledges the situation without attacking the person. Just avoid sarcasm, as it can backfire.

Humor reduces stress and can strengthen team dynamics, but knowing your audience is crucial. Practicing humorous responses in low-stakes situations can help others gain confidence in handling rude interactions with a bit of grace. The goal isn't to joke about everything but to use humor as a tool to defuse tension and create a lighter atmosphere.

Offering Emotional Support

While communication, boundaries, and humor are all helpful, offering emotional support can often be the most valuable. Dealing with rude people is exhausting, and sometimes, simple reassurance can make all the difference. After a tough day handling rude clients, just saying, "I'm here for you" or "That sounds really rough; let's talk about it" can be incredibly comforting.

Research shows that emotional support can reduce stress and help prevent long-term effects from repeated exposure to negativity (Social Connection Is the Strongest Protective Factor for Depression, 2020). Offering support doesn't have to be complicated; sometimes, just listening and validating their feelings is all someone needs. For example, if a friend comes to you upset after being treated poorly, acknowledging their frustration by saying, "I get why you're upset; that sounds so frustrating" can make them feel less isolated.

Sometimes, all someone needs is a listening ear and a bit of empathy to recharge. If emotional support alone isn't enough, offering to role-play difficult scenarios can give them the tools they need to manage these interactions more confidently. Let's look at how role-playing can help prepare for challenging situations.

Role-Playing Difficult Scenarios

Helping someone prepare for rude encounters requires practical strategies that build confidence and make it easier to respond with grace. The focus should be on four areas: choosing scenarios, practicing responses, providing feedback, and encouraging ownership. Each step helps equip people to handle rudeness calmly and confidently.

Scenario Selection

The first step is identifying situations where rudeness might come up. In a workplace, this might happen in meetings, emails, or customer interactions. Customer service workers, for example, deal with rude customers under pressure, while teachers may face challenging behavior from students or parents. Recognizing these scenarios helps people anticipate rude encounters and plan their responses.

Once you've identified scenarios, categorize the types of rudeness, from dismissive comments to overt hostility. Preparing responses for specific situations helps build confidence. Reflecting on past experiences is also helpful. Analyzing what worked and what didn't can make future encounters easier to manage.

Practice Sessions

Practicing responses builds confidence and reduces anxiety. Role-playing in a safe, simulated setting allows people to try different responses. For example, a colleague can pretend to be a demanding client while the person practices responding calmly and assertively.

Varying the scenarios ensures people learn how to handle different kinds of rudeness, from passive-aggressive comments to more direct hostility. This way, they're less likely to be caught off guard. Practicing in a low-pressure environment makes people feel more comfortable handling rudeness in real life. Adding a few unexpected elements, like a sudden escalation, can help them prepare for unpredictable situations.

Feedback and Growth

Feedback is crucial for growth. After practice, give balanced feedback that highlights strengths and areas for improvement. For example, you could acknowledge if someone stayed calm or used assertive body language, while also noting if they missed a chance to set boundaries.

Encouraging self-reflection is also valuable. Individuals can identify areas for improvement by reflecting on their responses. For instance, if they notice a tendency to get defensive, they can work on staying calm in future situations. Self-reflection helps improve emotional intelligence and keeps emotions in check.

Feedback should be actionable. If someone struggles to stay composed, suggesting deep breathing techniques can help them manage stress in the moment. Pausing before responding, as recommended by Harvard Business Review, can lead to more thoughtful reactions (Porath & Pearson, 2013). Regular feedback builds a culture of continuous learning and growth.

Encouraging Ownership

Ultimately, the goal is for individuals to take control of their responses to rudeness. Helping them understand that they can't control others' behavior but can control their own responses is key to building confidence. This involves focusing on emotional regulation and self-awareness, giving them a sense of control even in challenging situations.

Personal goals can help maintain motivation. For instance, someone might set a goal to stay calm in tense situations or use humor to diffuse tension. These goals encourage self-awareness and provide a roadmap for handling rude encounters effectively.

Understanding personal triggers is also essential. By identifying what triggers defensive or aggressive reactions, people can proactively manage them. Cognitive reframing, seeing rude behavior as a reflection of the other person's stress rather than a personal attack—can help reduce emotional responses and encourage calm reactions.

Positive self-talk is another helpful strategy. Reminding yourself that someone else's behavior is beyond your control can be empowering. Positive self-talk boosts resilience and keeps you focused under pressure.

Taking ownership means recognizing that while you can't control others, you can control your response. By encouraging this mindset, you're helping others build the confidence and resilience to handle rude encounters with grace.

Building skills to manage rudeness and creating a supportive environment are both essential. Let's talk about ways to foster a supportive environment for yourself and others.

Creating a Supportive Environment

Creating a supportive atmosphere, whether at work or in social circles, can make a big difference in how people handle rudeness. When people feel valued and supported, they're better equipped to manage negative interactions, which helps protect both their mental health and productivity. But a supportive environment doesn't just happen; it requires intentional steps to encourage open communication, positivity, clear expectations, and celebrating small wins. By making these small shifts, we can create a space where rude behaviors lose their impact and people feel more prepared to handle them.

Fostering Open Communication

Open communication is the foundation of a supportive environment. When people feel comfortable talking about rude behavior and how it affects them, they're less likely to let small issues build up and create long-term tension.

For example, teams could hold regular check-ins where members share experiences with rude behavior and discuss ways to handle it together. In these conversations, people can share coping tips, validate each other's feelings, and build resilience. In a work setting, this might mean setting aside a few minutes in meetings to address interpersonal issues or using anonymous surveys where team members can voice concerns without fear of judgment. Anonymous feedback can often reveal patterns of rudeness that might otherwise go unnoticed, giving managers the chance to address issues before they escalate.

Encouraging Positivity

Promoting a positive atmosphere is one of the best ways to counteract rudeness. When kindness and respect are the norms, rude behavior stands out and feels less acceptable. Plus, a positive environment boosts morale and makes people less likely to react rudely when they're stressed.

You can encourage positivity in simple ways. For example, try a "kindness challenge" where everyone is encouraged to do small acts of kindness, like helping a colleague with a task or offering encouragement. Studies show that small acts of kindness can lead to a 20% increase in team satisfaction and a 17% boost in productivity (Leading With Heart: The Revolutionary Impact of Kindness in Leadership, 2024). A little positivity doesn't just improve morale; it can also improve productivity.

Recognizing and rewarding positive behavior reinforces it, too. Appreciation emails or shout-outs during meetings are easy ways to boost morale. Team-building activities can also encourage collaboration and build trust. For instance, working together on a collaborative project can help people form stronger bonds, which reduces the likelihood of rude interactions. These activities help foster empathy and understanding, breaking down barriers and creating a more supportive environment.

Setting Ground Rules

Setting clear expectations is key to creating a supportive environment that minimizes rudeness. When everyone understands what's expected, it's easier to identify and address rude behavior if it happens.

One practical approach is creating a team charter or agreement with input from everyone involved. This document can outline expectations around respectful communication, constructive feedback, and even punctuality. When team members help create these guidelines, they're more likely to stick to them. It's not just about setting rules; it's about creating a shared understanding of what respect looks like in your group.

Clear expectations aren't just for work settings, they work in social environments too. In family settings, for example, setting guidelines about communication and how to handle disagreements can reduce the potential for rude exchanges and make everyone feel more comfortable.

Training in conflict resolution can also help set the tone. Learning how to navigate disagreements constructively, using active listening and empathy, reduces the chances that frustrations will turn into rude behavior. Teams with conflict resolution training tend to have fewer interpersonal conflicts and better dynamics overall.

Celebrating Small Wins

Celebrating small victories in respectful interactions reinforces positive behaviors and boosts morale. You don't need grand celebrations, small acknowledgments often mean the most. If a team manages a stressful project without anyone getting snappy, it's worth taking a moment to celebrate that.

Regularly recognizing these "wins" creates a cycle of positivity that encourages everyone to be more mindful of their behavior. For example, you could try a "win of the week" system, where you highlight someone who handled a tricky situation with professionalism and grace. Recognizing these wins not only motivates the individual but also sets a positive example for everyone else.

Research shows that celebrating small wins has big benefits. Studies have found that employees who regularly celebrate progress are more motivated and engaged (Nobel, 2011). Whether it's through a verbal acknowledgment, a quick email, or a small token of appreciation, recognizing these moments helps keep the atmosphere positive and encourages people to keep treating each other with respect.

Now that we've explored how a supportive environment can help manage rudeness, let's move on to the next step: building resilience. This is key to ensuring that when negativity comes your way, you can handle it with strength and grace.

Reflections

How can you empower others while protecting your own well-being by combining empathy, boundaries, and positivity in the face of difficult situations?

I've learned how essential emotional support is when dealing with difficult people. By encouraging others to express themselves without judgment, I can help them feel heard and relieve stress. Shifting focus to positivity has shown me that negative moments can be growth opportunities, building resilience and helping me find strength in even the most frustrating interactions. Setting clear boundaries has been another important takeaway—not only do boundaries protect my well-being, but they also teach others how to treat me with respect.

I've discovered that using humor carefully can ease tension, and practicing tough conversations through role-playing gives me the confidence to handle rude situations calmly. Celebrating small wins along the way creates a positive environment where respect and kindness can thrive. Now, I feel more empowered to manage rude encounters with empathy and strength, knowing that each one offers a chance to grow.

It's easy to feel overwhelmed or lose patience when dealing with rudeness and other frustrations. But with the right mindset and strategies, we can all find grace in those moments. Now, let's explore how we can apply this mindset to handle everyday annoyances with composure and kindness, even when it's tough.

15

FINDING GRACE IN EVERYDAY FRUSTRATIONS

"The greatest weapon against stress is our ability to choose one thought over another." – William James

I was juggling a dozen things at once, emailing, holding a mug, and listening to my daughter tell me about all of the princesses, when I dropped my phone, cracking the screen. I cursed under my breath, only to trip over the cat seconds later. In that frustrating moment, I had a choice: let the stress take over or laugh at the absurdity of it all. I chose laughter. Sweeping up the shards, I chuckled at the chaos, cat still underfoot, and carried on.

That small shift in perspective was a game-changer. Grace isn't about staying composed when life is smooth; it's about finding humor and calm when everything seems to go wrong. William James' words hold true here, choosing the right thought, even in the middle of a mess, is a powerful antidote to stress.

Moments like these make you question why we put so much pressure on ourselves to have everything under control. Life is messy, unpredictable, and sometimes downright ridiculous. But by embracing those imperfections with grace, we feel lighter, less stressed, and more resilient.

In this chapter, let's dive into how shifting your mindset can help you meet life's everyday annoyances with humor and composure. With a little grace, you'll find that even life's messiest moments can bring unexpected joy.

The Benefits of Grace

Choosing a gracious attitude can have a huge impact on your emotional well-being and relationships. Embracing grace, especially in moments of frustration, gives you a powerful tool for staying grounded and resilient. One of the first benefits of practicing grace is the boost it gives your emotional resilience. Grace becomes a buffer against the sting of rude encounters. For instance, if you're in a heated exchange with a coworker, taking a breath and responding with grace instead of reacting impulsively can ease the tension and keep stress from taking over. By not letting frustration control your response, you're setting the stage for more balanced emotions over time.

The more you practice responding gracefully in stressful situations, the stronger your ability to manage difficult emotions becomes. When grace becomes your go-to response, you're better prepared to handle frustrating moments with family, colleagues, or even strangers. Grace doesn't just soften a conflict in the moment—it builds your ability to stay calm and steady when life throws curveballs.

Another big benefit of grace is how it boosts your emotional intelligence. Choosing grace over anger helps you notice what triggers your emotions, making you more self-aware and giving you better control. For example, if a customer lashes out at you over something you can't control, it's easy to feel hurt or defensive. But with grace, you can see their frustration as separate from your performance, helping you stay composed. When you can separate your emotions from others', you show strong emotional intelligence. Practicing this over time makes it easier to handle tough interactions without letting them ruin your mood.

Grace also strengthens relationships. We all have moments where tension could escalate, but a gracious mindset can change the tone entirely. Think about a time you had a disagreement with a close friend that left both of you feeling unheard and frustrated. In moments like these, grace can shift the dynamic. Instead of pushing your point, try acknowledging their feelings first. By listening and validating their emotions, the conversation often moves in a positive direction. Grace encourages mutual respect and understanding, which leads to more productive and meaningful conversations.

Practicing grace isn't just beneficial for personal relationships; it's transformative in professional settings too. Imagine a work environment where people handle stress or disagreements with patience and understanding. Instead of sharp words, there's space for open communication and collaboration. A gracious attitude at work sets the stage for healthier, more productive relationships and builds trust and respect over time, benefiting everyone.

Grace also encourages personal growth and self-reflection. It allows you to step back and think about how you handle situations, and maybe how you could approach them differently. Let's say you had a challenging conversation with your supervisor, and it didn't go as smoothly as you'd hoped. Rather than focusing on your frustration, grace encourages you to reflect: Could you have been more patient or understanding? What lessons can you take away to make future interactions better? This kind of reflection is essential for personal growth, and grace can be the catalyst.

Regularly practicing grace can even nurture a growth mindset. Instead of seeing conflicts or setbacks as roadblocks, you start viewing them as chances to learn and improve. Over time, this mindset leads to greater emotional maturity and resilience, benefiting your personal and professional life.

Grace also has a positive ripple effect, creating more supportive environments at home or work. When you consistently show patience and understanding, even when things are challenging—you set a positive example for those around you. At work, for example, this might mean staying gracious when a colleague is stressed or a client is upset. Your calm, positive attitude can inspire others to respond similarly, creating a more collaborative and upbeat atmosphere.

In personal relationships, grace can be just as transformative. When you handle conflicts with empathy and understanding, you open the door to stronger connections, even when you disagree. A small gesture of grace can turn a heated argument into a chance for greater understanding and closeness.

An easy way to start practicing grace is by focusing on gratitude, which is closely tied to grace. Taking a moment to thank someone for their kindness or support strengthens your relationship and reinforces appreciation in your daily life. A great way to start is by writing a thank-you note. Whether it's to a colleague who helped you meet a deadline or a friend who lent a listening ear, sending them a note of appreciation can brighten their day and deepen your connection. Research by Dr. Robert A. Emmons and Dr. Michael E. McCullough shows that regularly practicing gratitude helps people develop a more positive outlook and boosts mental health (Stoerkel, 2019).

Now, let's dive into how to put these principles of grace into action and use them to respond thoughtfully when faced with everyday rudeness and conflict.

Graceful Responses in Action

Dealing with rude encounters isn't always easy, but learning how to respond with grace is a valuable skill. Using thoughtful words, nonverbal cues, and good timing, you can turn those frustrating moments into chances to grow. With a little practice, these strategies can help you stay composed and even de-escalate tense situations, whether you're at work, with family, or in social settings.

Verbal Responses

A calm, thoughtful response can quickly defuse rudeness. When someone makes a snide comment or snaps at you, choosing your words keeps the conversation civil. For example, if a co-worker criticizes you for missing a deadline, you might say, "I understand you're frustrated.

Let's discuss how we can move forward." When you recognize their emotions and focus on solutions, you keep the conversation productive and prevent the conflict from escalating.

Another effective tactic is asking clarifying questions. If someone makes a rude comment, you could ask, "Did you intend for that to come across as hurtful?" or "Can you explain what you meant by that?" This approach encourages the other person to reflect on their words without making them feel attacked. Asking for clarification can help the speaker rethink their behavior and lead to a more respectful conversation.

These verbal strategies can catch people off guard in a good way, prompting them to reconsider their tone. The aim isn't to embarrass anyone but to create an environment where respect becomes the priority, even in disagreements.

Non-Verbal Cues

Your body language can say a lot, even without words. How you carry yourself can either defuse or intensify a situation. Keeping your arms relaxed and maintaining a calm posture shows you're open and confident. Making gentle eye contact also conveys confidence, which can sometimes prompt the other person to rethink their behavior without you saying a word.

A small, genuine smile can also help ease the tension. Smiling (when it feels natural) shows you're composed and can even disarm someone who's being rude. But it's important to make sure the smile doesn't feel forced, as an inauthentic smile can come off as passive-aggressive. Nodding occasionally as they speak shows you're listening, which helps keep the interaction respectful. These nonverbal cues contribute to a calm atmosphere and can make a big difference in how the conversation goes.

Timing Your Responses

Timing is key when handling rudeness with grace. Our first reaction is often fueled by emotion, which can lead to a more heated exchange. Pausing for a moment gives you time to gather your thoughts and respond with a clear, calm mindset. Taking that beat prevents you from saying something you might regret and shows emotional maturity.

Sometimes, the best response is no response at all. Silence can be powerful, especially in professional settings. For example, if a client makes a sarcastic comment, pausing for a few seconds before replying shows that you're not rattled. This silence gives you a chance to decide if their remark even needs a response. Leadership expert Peter Bregman suggests a "four-second rule," where a brief pause helps you decide whether or not it's worth engaging (Bregman, n.d.).

In some situations, stepping back might be the most graceful choice. If you feel that responding will only make things worse, saying something like, "I need a moment to gather my thoughts. Let's come back to this later," can give everyone a chance to cool off and re-approach the conversation with a clearer mindset.

Taking a Step Back

Taking a step back, physically or mentally, can be incredibly helpful when dealing with rudeness. Sometimes, simply excusing yourself to regroup can help you handle the situation with more composure. This might be as simple as taking a deep breath or saying, "Let me think about this, and we can revisit it later." Stepping away signals that you're serious about resolving things without reacting emotionally.

This pause allows you and the other person a chance to reset, making it easier to approach the conversation with a clearer perspective.

Inspiring Stories of Grace

Real-life examples of handling rudeness with grace can be inspiring. These stories show us how staying calm and focusing on solutions can turn frustrating situations into something positive.

Take Sarah, one day, a customer started yelling about a billing issue. Instead of snapping back, Sarah calmly acknowledged their frustration, corrected the error, and even offered a small discount as a goodwill gesture. The customer, who had started off furious, ended up thanking her and leaving satisfied. Sarah's grace turned a negative experience into a positive one, earning the customer's loyalty.

Then there's John, who had a co-worker who constantly undermined him. During a team meeting, this co-worker openly criticized John's project. Instead of getting defensive, John thanked him for the feedback and suggested they collaborate to improve it. John's graceful response diffused the tension and turned the situation into a chance for teamwork.

Cultural and Influential Examples

Many cultures build grace right into their traditions. In Japan, the concept of "wa" focuses on creating harmony and avoiding conflict. Whether it's in a tea ceremony or everyday interactions, the goal is to create a peaceful, respectful experience. In South Africa, the principle of "Ubuntu" emphasizes community and compassion, showing that grace can be woven into the social fabric to promote respect and understanding.

Influential figures like Nelson Mandela and Mother Teresa also exemplify grace under pressure. After 27 years in prison, Mandela chose reconciliation over revenge, working to unite a divided South Africa. Mother Teresa, despite facing criticism, stayed dedicated to helping others with grace and humility. Their examples remind us that graceful responses can inspire positive change far beyond the immediate situation.

Handling rude encounters with grace is more than just a way to keep the peace in the moment, it builds emotional resilience, patience, and maturity. With time, staying composed in challenging interactions can become second nature, transforming how you approach life's inevitable frustrations.

Creating a positive environment supports and encourages interactions filled with grace. Let's look at how cultivating such environments can help you stay composed and bring out kindness in others.

Cultivating a Graceful Mindset

Developing a mindset that embraces grace in everyday situations takes effort and a genuine commitment to personal growth. Grace isn't just about being polite or friendly; it's about building an inner strength that allows you to respond calmly and thoughtfully, even when things or people get frustrating. Embracing this mindset means learning to manage your reactions rather than letting emotions take over. With a few practical strategies and intentional habits, you can start nurturing a more gracious outlook.

Self-Awareness Practices

The first step in building a gracious mindset is getting to know yourself and your triggers. Self-awareness helps you identify those comments or behaviors that tend to set you off and understand why they affect you. When you know what pushes your buttons, you're more prepared to respond thoughtfully instead of reacting on impulse.

A great way to boost self-awareness is by setting aside time for reflection. At the end of each day, take a few minutes to think about your interactions. Ask yourself questions like "Why did that comment bother me?" or "Could I have handled that situation differently?" This isn't about judging yourself; it's about understanding what's behind your reactions so you can respond more intentionally next time.

Another helpful technique is emotion charting. Track how you feel throughout the day to spot patterns in your emotions and physical responses. For example, if someone says something rude, do you feel tension in your shoulders or notice your heart racing? By observing these reactions, you'll start to recognize the signs that you're getting triggered, giving you a moment to pause and choose a calmer response. This simple awareness helps you regain control in situations that might otherwise throw you off balance.

Setting Intentions

Setting daily intentions is another way to cultivate grace. It doesn't have to be anything elaborate; just take a moment each morning to decide how you want to show up that day. An intention like "Today, I'll be patient no matter what" can be a mental anchor, preparing you to handle anything that might come your way.

Writing down your intention can make it even more powerful. Jot down something like "I'll approach all situations with kindness and empathy." This small act keeps your goal in mind throughout the day and serves as a reminder when you encounter frustrations. Making this a daily habit gradually builds a more positive, patient approach to life's ups and downs. It becomes easier to respond with grace, even if someone is being rude or difficult.

This practice can really change how you experience your day-to-day life. Instead of being blindsided by negativity or rudeness, you're prepared to handle them with patience and composure. It's like giving yourself an emotional buffer, so instead of reacting right away, you're choosing how you want to respond.

Community Engagement

The people around you play a huge role in helping you stay gracious. It's easier to stay positive and calm when you're with supportive, understanding people who value kindness. Whether it's family, friends, or colleagues, being around people who are patient and empathetic helps you mirror those qualities.

Look for communities that encourage positive communication and mutual support. Joining a book club, going to local meetups, or connecting with a professional network can introduce you to others who prioritize grace in their interactions. Activities that focus on cooperation and teamwork naturally strengthen your ability to handle challenging situations with patience. These interactions remind you that we're all working together, which makes it easier to practice kindness, even when things get tough.

Remember, you don't have to go it alone. Surrounding yourself with people who actively practice grace makes it so much easier to keep that mindset yourself. Their influence can inspire you and offer new perspectives on handling life's frustrations.

Reflection and Growth

Taking time to reflect on your actions helps you see how you're progressing, acknowledge your wins, and identify areas for growth. Regular reflection keeps you on track and strengthens your commitment to a gracious mindset. Being honest with yourself during this process is key to personal growth.

At the end of each week, take a moment to look back on how you interacted with others and handled different situations. Write down the moments you're proud of—those times when you stayed calm and handled things with grace. Also, jot down instances where you feel you could have done better. Focus on progress, not perfection. Every time you handle a frustrating situation with grace, you're taking a meaningful step forward.

You can also ask trusted friends, family, or colleagues for feedback on how you respond in challenging situations. Their insights can offer a fresh perspective and highlight things you might have missed. This feedback can be motivating, helping you keep improving.

Ongoing learning can also be a great tool for growth. Read books or articles on emotional intelligence and resilience, watch talks on handling conflict gracefully, or attend workshops on the subject. Learning from experts and real-world examples can give you new strategies and inspire you to keep refining your approach. Look to public figures or people you know who embody grace under pressure. Observing their behavior can give you ideas on what you can bring into your own life.

Remember, building a mindset of grace is an ongoing journey. The more you practice, the more naturally it becomes to handle rudeness and frustrations with calm and kindness. Over time, your reactions will shift from being automatic to thoughtful, making grace your default response.

Grace doesn't happen in isolation. It's much easier to keep a gracious mindset in a supportive environment. Next, let's explore how creating a positive atmosphere around you can strengthen and support your efforts to live with grace every day.

Creating a Positive Environment

Embracing grace in our personal and professional lives can transform these spaces into much more positive environments. Let's look at how this shift can happen in small, everyday ways.

Think about those times when someone's behavior is irritating or rude. It's natural to feel frustrated or even angry, but grace can turn these moments into lessons in kindness. Imagine a scenario where a co-worker unfairly criticizes your work. Instead of snapping back, responding with grace means calmly acknowledging their point of view and maybe even asking how you can help address their concerns. This not only eases the tension but also shows that you're choosing kindness over anger. Every challenging moment is a chance to practice patience and show understanding.

When you respond to tough situations with grace, you start to build a supportive environment around you. Graceful responses can set a positive example, inspiring others to act similarly. Imagine a workplace where handling mistakes with compassion is the norm instead of assigning blame. People would feel safe admitting errors and asking for help, knowing they'd receive support instead of criticism. This kind of positivity can have a ripple effect—showing kindness can inspire others to do the same, building a community based on mutual respect and empathy.

Starting with a positive attitude also sets the stage for uplifting interactions. It's simple but powerful: when you approach others with kindness and grace, you're more likely to get that same energy in return. For instance, if you start your day by greeting everyone with a smile or a kind word, chances are, your interactions will reflect that positivity throughout the day. People often mirror the energy we bring into conversations. This small shift doesn't just lift your own mood but helps create a space where positive interactions are the norm.

Grace also impacts how others see you. When you handle conflicts or tough situations with grace, it shows maturity and emotional intelligence. Colleagues, clients, and friends are more likely to respect and admire someone who stays calm and composed. This positive perception can lead to better relationships, deeper trust, and even new opportunities, both personally and professionally. People will naturally be drawn to you, knowing that your presence brings calm and solutions instead of stress.

One key to handling situations gracefully is using thoughtful language. Simple phrases can defuse tension and keep conversations respectful. For example, saying something like, "I understand why you might feel that way," shows empathy without escalating the situation. This response keeps the interaction on a positive track and can encourage a more constructive discussion. Practicing these phrases can make them feel natural over time, helping you maintain harmony in all kinds of interactions.

Humor can also be a powerful tool for handling rudeness. Sometimes, a well-timed joke can lighten the mood and shift a negative interaction into a moment of connection. If someone makes a snarky comment, responding with humor can redirect the conversation away from conflict. Used thoughtfully, humor doesn't downplay the issue but offers a fresh perspective, making it easier to handle the situation with grace.

When someone's being rude, asking a question like, "Can you help me understand what's bothering you?" can change the tone of the conversation. This question encourages both of you to pause, reflect, and steer the conversation toward solutions rather than focusing on the problem itself. It transforms a potentially confrontational moment into a chance for collaboration and understanding.

Expressing genuine curiosity about why someone might be acting rudely can be eye-opening. Often, people are rude because they're dealing with other frustrations. Showing a real interest in their perspective might help uncover the root of the behavior, creating an opportunity for honest communication. This approach humanizes the person and turns the interaction from a conflict into a meaningful conversation.

In personal relationships, practicing grace means looking beyond small irritations and focusing on the bigger picture. Instead of getting frustrated over a partner's or friend's little quirks, try to remember the many ways they contribute to your life and relationship. Focusing on the positives rather than the negatives helps build stronger, more resilient relationships.

In professional settings, grace can enhance teamwork and collaboration. Let's say you're working on a project, and a teammate misses a deadline. A gracious response would be to address the delay constructively, maybe asking if they faced any challenges and offering help if they need it. This approach not only resolves the issue but also fosters a supportive team environment, where everyone feels encouraged to support each other rather than assign blame.

The journey to embracing grace in everyday frustrations is ongoing. It requires self-awareness and a daily commitment to choose kindness over impulsive reactions. Reflecting on your day can help—think about moments when you responded with grace and areas where you could improve. This kind of reflection promotes growth and reinforces the goal of acting with grace.

Building a community that values and supports grace can also make a big difference. Surround yourself with people who inspire you to be your best self. Engage in conversations and activities that encourage kindness and understanding. Being part of a supportive community keeps you motivated to maintain grace in your actions and helps you stay focused on what truly matters.

Reflections

How can choosing grace in difficult moments help you not only grow personally but also inspire kindness and resilience in those around you?

In this chapter, I learned that choosing grace, especially in difficult moments, truly strengthens my emotional resilience. By responding with patience in conflicts, I build healthier relationships at home and at work, creating an atmosphere of kindness that can inspire others too.

Grace isn't only about staying calm; it's about showing others that kindness is always a choice. When faced with rude encounters, I realize that thoughtful responses and taking a pause can make all the difference.

Developing a gracious mindset requires me to stay self-aware and reflect on how I handle challenges, making adjustments as I go. The more I practice grace, the more I grow personally, and I see that I can bring positivity into my relationships and approach life with a lighter outlook.

Rude behavior can easily throw us off, but we don't have to let it ruin our day. By learning how to keep my peace in the face of negativity, I've gained confidence and strengthened my resilience. In the end, grace is a choice that helps me grow and brings more kindness into my world.

16

LIVING A LIFE FREE FROM THE ANNOYANCE OF RUDENESS

"Do not let the behavior of others destroy your inner peace." – Dalai Lama

I took my daughter to the her favorite "Big Park" to enjoy a wonderful afternoon outside when a younger couple walks by muttered something rude about my shoes. In that moment, I had two choices: react and let their rudeness ruin my mood, or shrug it off because, honestly, why should a random person's opinion affect me? I chose the latter, and it felt liberating to let their negativity roll off my shoulders. As the Dalai Lama reminds us, no one's behavior should have the power to rob us of our inner peace.

Moments like this remind me that choosing peace over irritation isn't just a one-time decision, it's a skill, a practice we can build over time. The more we let go of rude encounters, the stronger our ability to protect our peace becomes. And let's be honest, life's too short to give energy to every harsh comment or rude remark. In this chapter, we'll explore how consistent practice in letting go can transform how we navigate the world, keeping our inner calm intact no matter what life throws at us.

Consistency in Practice

Knowing how to handle rude encounters is only half the journey; the real challenge is putting these techniques into practice every day. Building a habit of responding positively doesn't happen overnight. It takes daily reminders, routines, regular check-ins, support from others, and gradual integration. But with consistency, you'll find that handling frustrations calmly becomes second nature.

Daily Reminders

One of the best ways to stay consistent is by setting up daily reminders to keep these techniques top of mind. A sticky note on your desk, a notification on your phone, or even a simple reminder to "breathe" can be a powerful nudge. Think of these as gentle cues to take a deep breath or to listen actively when confronted with rudeness. These little reminders can make a big difference over time.

Engaging with these reminders every day makes it easier to keep emotional management at the forefront, helping you avoid slipping into old habits. Whether it's a favorite quote that calms you or a phrase like "pause before you respond," these cues help reinforce your new habits. By adding reminders to your daily routine, you're giving yourself a boost to respond thoughtfully, even when you're in the thick of it.

Regular Check-Ins

Alongside reminders, regular check-ins can make a big difference in how well you stick to these new habits. These check-ins offer a chance to reflect on your interactions, celebrate what's going well, and see where you might need a little improvement.

A great way to do this is by journaling. Write down moments when you encountered rudeness, how you responded, and how you felt afterward. This gives you a clear picture of your progress over time. Reflecting in this way helps you notice patterns in your reactions and identify triggers, giving you more control over your responses.

These regular check-ins keep you actively involved in improving how you handle difficult situations. Think of it as having a personal meeting with yourself to assess your progress, celebrate small wins, and fine-tune your approach

Seeking Support

Handling rude behavior doesn't have to be a solo mission. Surrounding yourself with supportive friends, colleagues, or online groups can provide the encouragement and motivation you need to stay consistent. Sharing your experiences with others reminds you that you're not alone, and hearing how others deal with similar situations can offer fresh ideas and perspectives.

Talking about your challenges and successes reinforces your commitment to change. Sharing how you handled a rude encounter can boost your confidence and provide inspiration for others. This sense of camaraderie strengthens your resolve to keep practicing.

A support system can also bring in fresh viewpoints. Maybe a friend suggests a new approach, or a co-worker offers feedback on your strategies. Being part of a supportive community helps keep you engaged and encourages you to keep up the practice.

Gradual Integration

Consistency is key, but it's important not to overwhelm yourself with too many changes at once. Integrating new techniques gradually makes it easier to adapt and helps each one stick. Start by focusing on one technique at a time. For example, you might first practice deep breathing whenever you feel frustration building up. Once that feels natural, you can add another technique, like calmly setting boundaries.

Taking it one step at a time helps you build confidence. Every time you successfully apply a technique, it's a reminder that you can handle difficult situations without getting flustered. This steady progress keeps you from feeling overwhelmed and makes it easier to stay consistent. Focusing on one method at a time allows you to truly master each technique, creating a solid foundation for handling rudeness gracefully.

Now that you've put in the work to develop a consistent, calm response to rudeness, remember to celebrate your progress. Each small victory in managing difficult encounters deserves acknowledgment. Recognizing these little wins boosts your motivation and inspires you to keep moving forward on your journey.

Celebrating Small Victories

Recognizing and celebrating each step forward in managing your response to rudeness is a big part of personal growth. Even the smallest victories matter; they reinforce the positive changes you're making and keep you motivated to keep going. It's easy to brush off these little improvements, but they play a huge role in your journey to becoming more emotionally resilient. Take a moment to appreciate each step you've taken in handling rude interactions, and you'll see just how far you've come.

Recognition of Change

Noticing moments when you respond to rudeness with more calm or patience than before is the first step to celebrating your progress. Each time you realize you've reacted differently, maybe you shrugged off a rude comment that would've upset you before, you're proving that your efforts are paying off. That's real progress! Recognizing these shifts gives you a sense of accomplishment and shows you that the strategies you're using are making a difference.

Acknowledge these improvements as signs you're on the right path. Seeing the results of your hard work builds confidence that you can handle challenging situations in the future, which keeps you committed to growing even more. These moments don't just feel good in the short term; they strengthen your long-term commitment to responding with composure. The more you notice these small wins, the more you'll want to keep improving.

Celebrating All Wins, Big and Small

Celebrate progress by acknowledging more than just the significant achievements. Recognize each step of improvement, no matter how diminutive. More minor adjustments, like a subtle shift in your mindset, are just as necessary. Progress isn't always about dramatic changes, it's also about the little moments that signal you're moving in the right direction. For example, maybe you didn't react immediately to someone's rude comment or reframed a negative remark into something less personal. These might seem small, but they highlight essential shifts in your emotional resilience.

Recognizing these minor victories encourages you to see success from a broader perspective. Emotional growth takes time. It builds from small changes and steady effort. By being inclusive of all forms of progress, whether changing how you perceive rude interactions or responding, you can appreciate your journey thoroughly.

Celebrating various victories, even those that might seem trivial initially, helps create a positive mindset. You start to see that improvement is a process, not a single event. This makes self-improvement more achievable because you focus on steady, ongoing progress rather than waiting for one colossal breakthrough. By being inclusive of different types of achievements, you nurture a healthier outlook on growth and success.

Sharing Your Wins with Others

Sharing your victories with friends, family, or colleagues can make those accomplishments feel even more meaningful. Talking about the times you responded with patience or calm not only boosts your confidence but might inspire others to try the same. For example, if you tell a friend about handling a rude customer with patience, it may encourage them to use the same approach.

Celebrating your wins with others fosters a sense of support and understanding. When you share your progress, you contribute to a supportive community where everyone can celebrate each other's achievements. This shared experience is powerful; it's a reminder that you're not alone in working toward a better, more positive approach to dealing with difficult situations.

This supportive community creates a positive environment that reinforces the values you're working toward. When everyone around you is focused on celebrating progress, it becomes a motivating force for you. Knowing others are cheering you on strengthens your resolve to keep growing, and you, in turn, encourage them to celebrate their own successes. This culture of celebration fuels both personal growth and emotional resilience, making self-improvement feel like a team effort.

Practicing Gratitude

Adding gratitude to your celebrations can give them even more meaning. Focusing on what you're thankful for helps you shift your attention away from negative interactions and toward the positive aspects of your personal growth. This practice lets you appreciate your effort in managing your responses, making the whole journey more fulfilling.

Gratitude has a way of boosting emotional well-being. Taking a moment each day to list three things you're grateful for can shift your mindset and make it easier to let go of rude comments. When you focus more on what's going well than on what's going wrong, you naturally build emotional strength.

Regular gratitude practices create a resilient mindset. By focusing on the good things in your life, you develop emotional strength that helps you stay calm when faced with rudeness. Gratitude becomes a powerful tool for enhancing your emotional well-being, making it easier to brush off negativity. When gratitude is part of your routine, it acts as a buffer against the impact of rude behavior, helping you maintain your calm and composure.

Now that you're tuned in to celebrating these small victories, it's time to start thinking about building on your progress. Creating a plan for the long haul will help you keep developing the emotional resilience you've started and keep you on track for lasting personal growth. Let's dive into how to craft a plan that will keep you moving forward with confidence.

Creating a Long-Term Plan

Learning to handle rudeness doesn't happen overnight. It takes time, thoughtful planning, and a lot of practice and patience. Creating a long-term plan is key to dealing with rude behavior effectively and protecting your emotional well-being. This plan includes setting personal goals, regularly checking in to adjust your approach, trying out new techniques, and prioritizing self-care. With a bit of structure, you'll build resilience and learn to handle these challenging interactions calmly.

Defining Personal Goals

The first step is setting clear, specific goals for how you want to handle rude encounters. These goals are like a guide, helping you decide what kind of progress you want to see in how you respond emotionally. For instance, one goal might be staying calm when you usually feel irritated or defensive. Or maybe you want to respond to rudeness with kindness rather than sarcasm.

Defining these goals gives you a roadmap for improvement. When you know where you want to go, it's easier to track your progress and recognize when you've had a win. Each time you handle a rude interaction a little better than before, that's an achievement worth celebrating. These moments build confidence and encourage you to stay on track.

Having specific goals helps you focus on the areas where you want to grow, like learning to let go of negative comments or building emotional resilience. Clear objectives make it easier to work toward personal growth and see your improvement along the way.

Reviewing and Adjusting

Once you have your goals, it's important to regularly review and adjust your approach. Handling rudeness is a skill that evolves, and by checking in on your progress from time to time—whether monthly, quarterly, or yearly—you can keep growing and adapting your strategies.

Reflecting on your responses lets you spot any patterns. Are there particular triggers that make you more likely to react emotionally? Do specific types of rudeness bother you more than others? Noticing these patterns helps you fine-tune your plan. For instance, if you tend to lose your cool when interrupted, you can focus on staying calm in those situations.

Long-term success requires flexibility. Your plan shouldn't be set in stone but should be something you can adjust as you grow. Staying open to change means you can keep refining your approach and improve over time. What works for you today might need tweaking down the road, so be prepared to adapt as you continue on your journey.

Trying New Strategies

As you practice handling rude encounters, staying open to new techniques can help you keep growing. Learning how to deal with difficult situations is an ongoing process, and adding fresh approaches can keep you moving forward. This might mean exploring new resources like books, articles, or even workshops on emotional intelligence or communication skills. Each new insight adds another tool to your toolbox.

For example, if you're working on staying calm, you might discover new approaches, like using humor to lighten the mood or practicing active listening to de-escalate tense situations. Keeping your approach dynamic ensures you're always building new skills to handle whatever comes your way.

Learning from others is also valuable. Whether it's through formal training or just chatting with friends and colleagues about how they manage difficult interactions, hearing different perspectives can give you fresh ideas. Adding new strategies to your plan means you're constantly evolving in how you approach rudeness.

Making Time for Self-Care

Prioritizing self-care is one of the most important parts of your long-term plan. Managing rude behavior can be emotionally draining, and without caring for yourself, burnout can creep up fast. Regular self-care helps you stay strong and maintain the mental energy needed to handle challenging interactions.

Integrating self-care into your routine gives you a clear perspective and helps you approach tough situations with a calm mind. Whether it's taking short breaks, practicing relaxation techniques, or doing things you enjoy, self-care is essential for emotional well-being.

If you often deal with rude customers or colleagues, stepping away for a few minutes to recharge can help you return with a clearer head. And engaging in hobbies or activities outside of work that bring you joy can boost your emotional resilience, making it easier to let rude comments roll off and stay focused on the positives.

Self-care doesn't have to take a lot of time. Even small acts, like taking a few deep breaths during a stressful moment or spending five minutes journaling at the end of the day, can make a big difference in how you feel. These small practices help you bounce back from emotionally tough situations and improve how you respond in the future.

Now that you have a plan in place, take some time to reflect on how far you've come. Recognizing your progress is a big part of building emotional resilience and staying motivated on your journey. Let's look at how celebrating personal transformation can keep you moving forward with confidence.

Reflecting on Personal Transformation

Taking a moment to reflect on how much you've grown in handling rudeness can be incredibly rewarding. Looking back at your journey reveals the progress you've made, from the lessons you've picked up along the way to the emotional resilience you've built. This reflection not only helps you see how far you've come but also prepares you to tackle future challenges with even more grace.

Using a Reflection Journal

One of the best ways to capture your growth is by keeping a reflection journal. Writing down your experiences and feelings helps you become more aware of the changes you've gone through. Journaling lets you process your emotions and understand how you respond to rude encounters on a deeper level.

When you look back at your entries, you'll see your journey unfold. Maybe there was a time when a single rude comment would've ruined your entire day, but now you can brush it off without a second thought. Regularly reflecting on your progress allows you to spot patterns and triggers, making it easier to see where you've improved and where there's still room to grow.

Identifying Key Learnings

As you reflect, try to identify the key takeaways from your experiences with rudeness. These insights are proof of your growth and show you just how far you've come.

Think about which strategies worked best for you and which didn't. Maybe staying calm and silent helped in a heated moment, or perhaps setting boundaries made all the difference. Understanding what worked gives you a clear path forward and helps you refine your approach for future situations. These lessons act as a roadmap, reminding you that your growth is an ongoing journey.

Sharing Growth Stories

Sharing your transformation with others can be incredibly inspiring, not just for you but for those around you. Talking about your journey with friends, family, or colleagues can create a stronger sense of connection and understanding. It's reassuring to hear that others have faced similar challenges and grown through them.

Sharing your story can also encourage others to reflect on their own experiences and growth. Sometimes, you'll gain new insights or strategies from these conversations that you hadn't considered before. Creating a space where everyone can share their growth builds a supportive community where each person feels motivated by everyone's progress.

Fostering a Growth Mindset

Growth doesn't happen all at once; it's a gradual, ongoing process. Adopting a growth mindset helps you see each challenge as an opportunity to learn and improve. This perspective encourages resilience, allowing you to approach rudeness and other tough situations with curiosity instead of frustration.

When you commit to growth, you stay adaptable and open-minded. You understand that personal development is a lifelong journey—one where you're always learning, evolving, and improving. This mindset not only helps you handle rudeness with grace but also empowers you to grow in every area of your life.

Reflections

What daily habits or reminders can you implement to help you protect your peace and build emotional resilience when faced with negativity?

I've realized that I have the power to protect my peace by choosing how I respond to negativity. Daily reminders keep me grounded, helping me focus on managing my emotions, and regular check-ins allow me to track my progress and see where I can improve. Taking things step-by-step has been key; it prevents being overwhelmed and makes growth feel achievable. Celebrating small wins, like staying calm during a rude encounter, boosts my confidence and reminds me that these changes are real.

Prioritizing self-care has become more important than ever. It's not just about feeling good; it's about building the emotional strength to handle whatever comes my way. Adopting a growth mindset helps me embrace every challenge as a chance to learn. I'm not just handling rudeness, I'm building resilience, one habit at a time.

Through consistent practice, celebrating small wins, and leaning on a support network, I'm finding more freedom from the annoyance of rudeness. This journey has shown me that every choice I make to stay calm, reflect, and grow brings me closer to a stronger, more peaceful version of myself.

17

CONCLUSION

"You cannot control the behavior of others, but you can always choose how you respond to it." – Roy T. Bennett

Asking ourselves "Why do rude people piss me off?" has taken us on a deep dive into the roots of rudeness, helping us understand why people sometimes act in ways that frustrate or even hurt us. By exploring our experiences and identifying common triggers, we've uncovered valuable insights into why disrespectful behavior happens and how it affects us. With these insights, we've learned practical techniques like pausing, breathing, and choosing thoughtful responses to stay centered when we encounter rudeness.

One powerful takeaway has been the ability to use humor as a tool. Seeing the humor in rudeness can transform frustrating moments into opportunities for laughter and connection. Humor defuses tension and builds resilience, helping us face rudeness with confidence rather than frustration. Those who can laugh at the absurdity often come out stronger, feeling more grounded and prepared for the next encounter.

We've also seen how essential setting boundaries is for dealing with rudeness effectively. Establishing limits not only protects us but enhances relationships by creating a space for mutual respect. When we communicate clearly about what we find acceptable and what we don't, we're creating an environment that prioritizes understanding over tension. Boundaries become a powerful form of self-care, helping us manage interactions without absorbing unnecessary stress.

Personal growth is a lifelong process, and building resilience to rudeness is no different. The art of responding to rudeness with grace is a skill we can continue to develop. Journaling, for instance, lets us reflect on complex interactions, while input from trusted friends and mentors provides encouragement and fresh perspectives. Every small win—like staying calm during a tense moment—is worth celebrating because it reinforces positive habits and boosts our confidence. These steps create lasting change, helping us handle life's little annoyances more effectively.

Keeping a positive outlook is a guiding light through life's challenges. When we embrace gratitude, we shift our focus from what's bothering us to what's going well. As Martin Luther King Jr. wisely said, "Darkness cannot drive out darkness; only light can do that." Cultivating gratitude for the good things in life helps us stay centered, even in the face of rudeness. Positivity isn't about ignoring negativity; it's about choosing to let the good outweigh the bad.

Mastering the art of handling rudeness takes practice, reflection, and a commitment to growth. Every encounter offers a chance to refine our responses, whether it's through pausing to breathe, injecting humor, setting boundaries, or maintaining a positive outlook. Each small action builds a more resilient, adaptable mindset.

Reflecting on this journey, I realize that mastering our reactions isn't about perfection—it's about progress. Remember that sarcastic stranger in the bookstore? If I met them today, I'd probably laugh even harder and feel lighter even faster. That's the real power of choosing how we respond.

As you reflect on the stories we've shared, remember that we all face rude moments. But the way we handle these encounters can define how we navigate the world. Choosing a proactive approach rather than a reactive one empowers us to handle rudeness with grace and composure.

You're now equipped to deal calmly and confidently with rude encounters, whether they come from a colleague, client, or stranger. Understanding that rudeness often stems from stress or insecurity can help you respond with empathy rather than frustration. This journey isn't about perfection—it's about continued growth. Keep practicing, be open to new techniques, and celebrate every small victory.

Final Reflection:

So, as you close this book, I invite you to put these tools into practice, one interaction at a time. Let's transform life's little annoyances into opportunities for growth, connection, and maybe even a good laugh. Here's to a more peaceful, joyful you!

Ultimately, learning to handle rudeness isn't just about protecting your peace; it's about creating a happier, more constructive space for yourself and those around you. Every positive action you take has a ripple effect, inspiring those around you to respond to life's frustrations with respect and kindness. Embrace each encounter as a chance to practice, grow, and connect. Here's to mastering the art of handling life's little annoyances with a sense of humor, empathy, and grace!

THANKS FOR READING!

If you've made it this far, I just want to say thank you. Seriously, thank you for giving this book your time and energy.

If you found value here, I think you'll love my next one.

🔥 Ready to Keep Growing?

My new book, *Mental Toughness Training Made Simple*, is packed with practical tools to help you build resilience, handle stress, and take back control of your mindset.

📱 Tap into your next level. Mental clarity, discipline, and focus start here.

📲 Scan the QR code or click the link below to grab your copy:

👉 CLICK HERE

Thanks for Reading!

Michael T. Bennett

Author of *Why Do Rude People Piss Me Off and Mental Toughness Training Made Simple.*

P.S. Keep an eye out for more tips and insights in the future. We'd love to stay connected! 😊

Thanks for Reading!

This Isn't the End. It's the Moment That Matters.

You've finished the book. You've shown up for yourself.

Now I'm asking you to show up for me.

Writing this wasn't easy. It came from a place of hard-won lessons, long nights, and a real belief that mental toughness can change lives. It changed mine.

But I'm not backed by a big publisher. I don't have a marketing machine behind me. I have this. You.

If this book helped you, I'm asking genuinely for your help in return.

Thanks for Reading!

Leave a review. Tell someone why it mattered. Your words could be the reason someone else decides to invest in their mindset too.

My work, my future, my ability to keep doing this, it depends on readers like you.

Scan the QR code or Click Here and be part of the story.

REFERENCES

Adams-Colon, B. (2021, June 23). *The simple act of stretching*. Colorado State University. https://www.research.colostate.edu/healthyagingcenter/2021/06/23/the-simple-act-of-stretching/

Adult Activity: An overview. (2023, December 20). CDC. https://www.cdc.gov/physical-activity-basics/guidelines/adults.html

Angelou, M. (2011). *The complete collected poems of Maya Angelou*. Random House LLC.

Baer, M. B. (2017, February 28). *Empathy is the key to conflict resolution or management*. Psychology Today. https://www.psychologytoday.com/us/blog/empathy-and-relationships/201702/empathy-is-the-key-conflict-resolution-or-management

Baikie, K. A., & Wilhelm, K. (2005). Emotional and physical health benefits of expressive writing. *Advances in Psychiatric Treatment, 11*(5), 338-346. https://www.cambridge.org/core/journals/advances-in-psychiatric-treatment/article/emotional-and-physical-health-benefits-of-expressive-writing/ED2976A61F5DE56B46F07A1CE9EA9F9F

Bennett, R. T. (2016). *The light in the heart*. Roy T. Bennett.

Benson, K. (2024, September 18). *The magic relationship ratio, according to science*. The Gottman Institute. https://www.gottman.com/blog/the-magic-relationship-ratio-according-science/

Bergland, C. (2022, October 30). *Why quick bursts of vigorous activity are a game-changer*. Psychology Today. https://www.psychologytoday.com/us/blog/the-athletes-way/202210/why-quick-bursts-vigorous-activity-are-game-changer

Blachnio, A. (2021). Be happy, be honest: The role of self-control, self-beliefs, and satisfaction with life in honest behavior. *Journal of Religion and Health, 60*(2), 1015-1028. https://pubmed.ncbi.nlm.nih.gov/31797252/

Bregman, P. (n.d.). *Four seconds: all the time you need to stop counter-productive habits and get the results you want*. FluidSelf. https://fluidself.org/books/self-help/four-seconds

Brown, B. (2010). *The Gifts of Imperfection: Let Go of Who You Think You're Supposed to Be and Embrace Who You Are*. Hazelden Publishing

Carnegie, D. (1936). *How to Win Friends and Influence People*. Simon & Schuster.

Cascio, C. N., O'Donnell, M. B., Tinney, F. J., Libberman, M. D., Taylor, S. E., Strecher, V. J., & Falk, E. B. (2016, April). Self-affirmation activates brain systems associated with self-related processing and reward and is reinforced by future orientation. *Social Cognitive and Affective Neuroscience, 11*(4), 621-629. https://academic.oup.com/scan/article/11/4/621/2375054?login=false

Cherry, K. (2023, March 10). *Individualistic culture: Definition, traits, and examples*. Verywell Mind. https://www.verywellmind.com/what-are-individualistic-cultures-2795273

Cherry, K. (2023, May 4). *Positive thinking: Definition, benefits, and how to practice*. Verywell Mind. https://www.verywellmind.com/what-is-positive-thinking-2794772

References

Chowdhury, M. R. (2019, April 9). *The neuroscience of gratitude and effects on the brain.* PositivePsychology.com. https://positivepsychology.com/neuroscience-of-gratitude/

Cohen, I. S. (2023, November 13). *Understanding bowen family systems theory.* Psychology Today. https://www.psychologytoday.com/us/blog/your-emotional-meter/202311/understanding-bowen-family-systems-theory

Cohen, P. (2001, November 21). *Mental gymnastics increase bicep strength.* NewScientist. https://www.newscientist.com/article/dn1591-mental-gymnastics-increase-bicep-strength/

Covey, S. R. (1989). *The 7 Habits of Highly Effective People: Powerful Lessons in Personal Change.* Free Press.

Creswell, J. D., Dutcher, J. M., Klein, W. M.P., Harris, P. R., & Lavine, J. M. (2013, May 1). Self-affirmation improves problem-solving under stress. *PLOS One.* https://journals.plos.org/plosone/article?id=10.1371/journal.pone.0062593

Crowley, M. C. (2018, October 27). *Dr. Christine Porath: Workplace incivility requires a leadership fix.* Mark C. Crowley. https://markccrowley.com/dr-christine-porath-workplace-incivility-requires-a-leadership-fix/

Dalai Lama. (n.d.). *Do not let the behavior of others destroy your inner peace.*

Davis, T. (2023, November 20). *How visualization can benefit your well-being.* Psychology Today. https://www.psychologytoday.com/intl/blog/click-here-for-happiness/202308/how-visualization-can-benefit-your-well-being

Dora, J. (2019, November 15). *Why do we experience fatigue?* Psychology Today. https://www.psychologytoday.com/us/blog/on-human-decision-making/201911/why-do-we-experience-fatigue

Dreher, D. E. (2019, June 11). *Why talking about our problems makes us feel better.* Psychology Today. https://www.psychologytoday.com/us/blog/your-personal-renaissance/201906/why-talking-about-our-problems-makes-us-feel-better

Dyer, W. (2009). *Excuses Begone!: How to Change Lifelong, Self-Defeating Thinking Habits.* Hay House.

Ede, D. E., Walter, F. A., & Hughes, J. W. (2020, March 6). Exploring how trait mindfulness relates to perceived stress and cardiovascular reactivity. *International Journal of Behavioral Medicine, 27,* 415-425. https://link.springer.com/article/10.1007/s12529-020-09871-y

Edwards, E. (2010). Resilience and acceptance. Beacon Press.

Everything you need to know about progressive muscle relaxation. (2022, November 10). Cleveland Clinic | Health Essentials. https://health.clevelandclinic.org/progressive-muscle-relaxation-pmr

Frankl, V. E. (1959). *Man's Search for Meaning.* Beacon Press.

Fuller, K. (2023, August 21). *How clutter and mental health are connected.* Verywell Mind. https://www.verywellmind.com/decluttering-our-house-to-cleanse-our-minds-5101511

Gracián, B. (1647). The Art of Worldly Wisdom.

Green spaces may boost wellbeing for city dwellers. (2013, April 22). University of Exeter. https://news-archive.exeter.ac.uk/featurednews/title_281065_en.html

Grossman, S. (n.d.). *From threats to challenges: How to reframe your mindset for greater motivation and resilience.* Warrior Publishing. https://drsharongrossman.com/from-

References

threats-to-challenges-how-to-reframe-your-mindset-for-greater-motivation-and-resilience/

Hanson, R. (2021, September 14). *Why the tone of your voice makes such a difference.* Psychology Today. https://www.psychologytoday.com/us/blog/your-wise-brain/202109/why-the-tone-your-voice-makes-such-difference

How to increase productivity by 21% with employee engagement. (2024, February 7). Applauz. https://www.applauz.me/resources/how-employee-engagement-increases-productivity

James, W. (2013). *The Principles of Psychology (Vol. 1).* Dover Publications. (Original work published 1890)

Japanese bowing: etiquette and meanings: Apologies and greetings in Japan. (2020, October 21). Kanpai. https://www.kanpai-japan.com/japan-lifestyle/japanese-bowing-etiquette-meanings

Jerath, R., Crawford, M. W., Barnes, V. A., & Harden, K. (2015, April 14). Self-regulation of breathing as a primary treatment for anxiety. *Applied Psychophysiology and Biofeedback, 40,* 107-115. https://link.springer.com/article/10.1007/s10484-015-9279-8

Krakovsky, M. (2017, September 20). *Why mindset matters.* Stanford Magazine. https://stanfordmag.org/contents/why-mindset-matters

Leading with heart: The revolutionary impact of kindness in leadership. (2024, April 4). AgileIdeation. https://agile-ideation.com/blog/2024/4/4/leading-with-heart-the-revolutionary-impact-of-kindness-in-leadership

Lee, M.-S., Lee, J., Park, B.-J., & Miyazaki, Y. (2015). Interaction with indoor plants may reduce psychological and physiological stress by suppressing autonomic nervous system activity in young adults: a randomized crossover study. *Journal of Physiological Anthropology, 34.* https://jphysiolanthropol.biomedcentral.com/articles/10.1186/s40101-015-0060-8

Mackay, H. (2008). *Use Your Head to Get Your Foot in the Door: Job Search Secrets No One Else Will Tell You.* Penguin Group.

Manage stress: Strengthen your support network. (2022, October 21). American Psychological Association. https://www.apa.org/topics/stress/manage-social-support

Marcinek, L. (2024, January 29). *Using the five senses.* ADAA. https://adaa.org/living-with-anxiety/personal-stories/using-five-senses

Marone, L. (2021, June 27). *Resilience: The power to overcome, adjust, and persevere.* Psychology Today. https://www.psychologytoday.com/us/blog/gaining-and-sustaining/202106/resilience-the-power-overcome-adjust-and-persevere

Mårtensson, J. (n.d.). *Feelings are much like waves.* [Quote].

Martin, S. (2022, September 16). *How better boundaries can prevent burnout.* Psychology Today. https://www.psychologytoday.com/us/blog/conquering-codependency/202209/how-better-boundaries-can-prevent-burnout

Melville, H. (1851). *Moby-Dick; or, The Whale.* Richard Bentley.

Meneghel, I., Salanova, M., & Martinez, I. M. (2014, November 7). Feeling good makes us stronger: how team resilience mediates the effect of positive emotions on team performance. *Journal of Happiness Studies, 17,* 239-255. https://link.springer.com/article/10.1007/s10902-014-9592-6

Neumann, R.J., Ahrens, K.F., Kollman, B., Goldbach, N., Chmitorz, A., Weichert, D.,

References

Fiebach, C.J., Wessa, M., Kalisch, R., Lieb, K., Tuscher, O., Plichta, M.M., Reif, A., & Matura, S. (2022). The impact of physical fitness on resilience to modern life stress and the mediating role of general self-efficacy. *European Archives of Psychiatry and Clinical Neuroscience, 272*, 679-692. https://link.springer.com/article/10.1007/s00406-021-01338-9

NeuroLaunch Editorial Team. (2024, August 18). *Visualization for relaxation and stress reduction: Harnessing its power*. NeuroLaunch. https://neurolaunch.com/how-does-visualization-promote-relaxation-and-stress-reduction/

Nobel, C. (2011, September 6). *How small wins unleash creativity*. Harvard Business School. https://hbswk.hbs.edu/item/how-small-wins-unleash-creativity

Nonviolence. (n.d.). Stanford | The Martin Luther King, Jr. Research and Education Institute. https://kinginstitute.stanford.edu/nonviolence

Obama, M. (2016, July 25). Remarks at the Democratic National Convention. Philadelphia, PA. https://obamawhitehouse.archives.gov/the-press-office/2016/07/25/remarks-first-lady-democratic-national-convention

The outsized impacts of rudeness in the workplace. (2021, June 22). Carnegie Mellon University. https://www.cmu.edu/tepper/news/stories/2021/june/workplace-rudenesss-study.html

Porath, C. (2017, September 27). *The incivility bug*. Psychology Today. https://www.psychologytoday.com/us/blog/thriving-at-work/201709/the-incivility-bug

Porath, C., & Pearson, C. (2013). *The price of incivility*. Harvard Business Review. https://hbr.org/2013/01/the-price-of-incivility

Price, M. (2018, March 14). *Goal-setting is linked to higher achievement*. Psychology Today. https://www.psychologytoday.com/us/blog/the-moment-youth/201803/goal-setting-is-linked-higher-achievement

Rhodes, J. (2024, February 27). *The science behind imagery and visualisation*. Psychology Today. https://www.psychologytoday.com/us/blog/imagery-coaching/202402/the-science-behind-imagery-and-visualisation

Roggero, V. (2023, November 22). *Setting boundaries: A crucial aspect of mental wellness*. Vivien Roggero. https://vivienroggero.com/blog/setting-boundaries-a-crucial-aspect-of-mental-wellness

Ryskin, R. A., Benjamin, A. S., Tullis, J., & Brown-Schimdt, S. (2015). Perspective-taking in comprehension, production, and memory: An individual differences approach. *Journal of Experimental Psychology: Genera, 144*(5), 898-915. https://psycnet.apa.org/record/2015-33089-001

Sarcasm is lost on the older generation. (2016, January 5). University of Aberdeen. https://www.abdn.ac.uk/news/8567/

Sehat, P. (2023, September 13). *The power of I statements: Communicating effectively*. Well Beings Counselling. https://wellbeingscounselling.ca/the-power-of-i-statements/

Seneca. (n.d.). "Luck is what happens when preparation meets opportunity."

Seven or more hours of sleep per night: A health necessity for adults. (2024, July 30). AASM. https://aasm.org/seven-or-more-hours-of-sleep-per-night-a-health-necessity-for-adults/

Shaw, G. B. (n.d.). *The single biggest problem in communication is the illusion that it has taken place [Quote]*. GoodReads. Retrieved from. https://www.goodreads.com/quotes/5463-the-single-biggest-problem-in-communication-is-the-illusion

Shpancer, N. (2020, December 9). *A science-based technique for coping with stress*.

References

Psychology Today. https://www.psychologytoday.com/us/blog/insight-therapy/202012/science-based-technique-coping-stress

Smith, D. B. (2018, October 24). *Power of the mind: The science of visualization*. Science Abbey. https://www.scienceabbey.com/2018/10/24/power-of-the-mind-the-science-of-visualization-1/

Smyth, J. M., Johnson, J. A., Auer, B. J., Lehman, E., Talamo, G., & Sciamanna, C. N. (2018). Online positive affect journaling in the improvement of mental distress and well-being in general medical patients with elevated anxiety symptoms: A preliminary randomized controlled trial. *JMIR Mental Health*, *5*(4). https://mental.jmir.org/2018/4/e11290/

Social connection is the strongest protective factor for depression. (2020, August 14). ScienceDaily. https://www.sciencedaily.com/releases/2020/08/200814131007.htm

Stoerkel, E. (2019, February 4). *The science and research on gratitude and happiness*. Positive Psychology. https://positivepsychology.com/gratitude-happiness-research/

Stone, K. (2023, December 2). *The impact of employee engagement on productivity*. Engagedly. https://engagedly.com/blog/impact-of-employee-engagement-on-productivity/

Walsh, K. (2023, January 14). *The best walking plan to reduce stress*. EatingWell. https://www.eatingwell.com/article/8024858/walking-plan-to-reduce-stress/

Weger, H. J., Bell, G. C., Minei, E. M., & Robinson, M. C. (2014, January 8). The relative effectiveness of active listening in initial interactions. *International Journal of Listening*, *28*(1), 13-31. https://www.tandfonline.com/doi/full/10.1080/10904018.2013.813234

Whitbourne, S. K. (2024, May 10). *Why sarcasm can seriously damage a relationship*. Psychology Today. https://www.psychologytoday.com/us/blog/fulfillment-at-any-age/202404/keep-the-sarcasm-in-check-to-keep-your-relationship-alive

Winfrey, O. (2019). *The path made clear: Discovering your life's direction and purpose*. Flatiron Books.

Yu, A., Berg, J. M., & Zlatev, J. J. (2021, May). Emotional acknowledgment: How verbalizing others' emotions fosters interpersonal trust. *Organizational Behavior and Human Decision Processes*, *164*, 116-135. https://www.sciencedirect.com/science/article/abs/pii/S0749597821000194

Printed in Dunstable, United Kingdom